Whenever

Alan Ayckbourn, Artistic Director of the Stephen Joseph Theatre, Scarborough, was born in London in 1939. He has worked in theatre all his life as, variously, stage manager, sound technician, lighting technician, scene painter, propmaker, actor, writer and director. Most of these talents he developed (or abandoned) thanks to his mentor and founder of the theatre in Scarborough, Stephen Joseph, who first encouraged him to write and after whom the theatre is named. Almost all of the sixty-one plays Alan Ayckbourn has written to date received their first performance at this theatre. Over half have subsequently been produced in the West End, at the Royal National Theatre or the Royal Shakespeare Company. Translated into thirty languages, they have been seen on stage and television throughout the world receiving many national and international awards. Alan Ayckbourn was appointed a CBE in 1987, and in 1997 became the first playwright to be knighted since Terence Rattigan. A new trilogy, *Damsels in Distress*: *GamePlan*, *FlatSpin*, *RolePlay*, premièred at the Stephen Joseph Theatre in 2001 and transferred to the West End in September 2002, coinciding with the publication of his book *The Crafty Art of Playmaking*.

by the same author

plays
WOMAN IN MIND (DECEMBER BEE)
MR A'S AMAZING MAZE PLAYS
INVISIBLE FRIENDS
THE REVENGERS' COMEDIES
TIME OF MY LIFE
WILDEST DREAMS
COMMUNICATING DOORS
THINGS WE DO FOR LOVE
COMIC POTENTIAL
THE BOY WHO FELL INTO A BOOK
HOUSE AND GARDEN

DAMSELS IN DISTRESS TRILOGY
(*GamePlan, FlatSpin, RolePlay*)

ALAN AYCKBOURN: PLAYS ONE
(*A Chorus of Disapproval, A Small Family Business,
Henceforward..., Man of the Moment*)

ALAN AYCKBOURN: PLAYS TWO
(*Ernie's Incredible Illucinations, Invisible Friends,
This Is Where We Came in, My Very Own Story,
The Champion of Paribanou*)

adaptations
THE FOREST by Alexander Ostrovsky

theatre books
THE CRAFTY ART OF PLAYMAKING

ALAN AYCKBOURN

Whenever

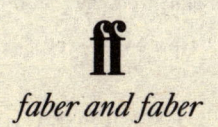

ff
faber and faber

First published in 2002
by Faber and Faber Limited
3 Queen Square London WC1N 3AU
Published in the United States by Faber and Faber Inc.
an affiliate of Farrar, Straus and Giroux LLC, New York

Typeset by Country Setting, Kingsdown, Kent CT14 8ES
Printed in England by Mackays of Chatham plc, Chatham, Kent

All rights reserved

© Haydonning Ltd, 2002
Music © Denis King, 2002

The right of Alan Ayckbourn and Denis King (music)
to be identified as authors of this work has been asserted
in accordance with Section 77 of the Copyright,
Designs and Patents Act 1988

All rights whatsoever in this work, amateur or professional,
are strictly reserved. Applications for permission for any use
whatsoever including professional performance rights must be
made in advance, prior to any such proposed use, to
Casarotto Ramsay and Associates Ltd, National House,
60–66 Wardour Street, London W1V 4ND and ML 2000 Ltd.,
Douglas House, 16–18 Douglas Street, Westminster,
London SW1P 4PB. Amateur applications for permission to
perform, etc., must be made in advance, before rehearsals begin,
to Samuel French Ltd., 52 Fitzroy Street, London W1P 6JR.
No performance may be given unless a licence has first
been obtained.

*This book is sold subject to the condition that it shall not, by way
of trade or otherwise, be lent, resold, hired out or otherwise
circulated without the publisher's prior consent in any form of
binding or cover other than that in which it is published and
without a similar condition including this condition being
imposed on the subsequent purchaser*

A CIP record for this book
is available from the British Library

ISBN 0-571-21508-4

2 4 6 8 10 9 7 5 3 1

Whenever was first performed at the Stephen Joseph Theatre, Scarborough, on 5 December 2000. The cast was as follows:

Emily Alison Pargeter
Mrs Binns, Mrs Green, Guest at Party, The Time Keeper
  Sarah Redmond
Clara aged 12, Minnie, Guest at Party, Char Tee
  Saskia Butler
Charity aged 30, Clara aged 66, Droid 1 Nicola Sloane
Lucas aged 34, Lucas aged 88, Droid 2 Richard Banharn
Bob, George, Chauffeur, Vocalist/Guest at Party, Ziggi
  Giles Taylor
Woolton, Mr Green, Guest at Party, Hoombean
  Nigel Williams
Martin, Bill, Nigel Chatterton-Brown, Droid 3
  Stefan Bednarczyk
Oscar Gavin Lee

Director Alan Ayckbourn
Designer Roger Glossop
Lighting Designer Mick Hughes
Costume Designer Christine Wall
Musical Director Simon Cryer
Choreographer Gavin Lee

Characters

IN VICTORIAN TIMES

Emily Bonny
a nine-year-old girl

Lucas Lashmore
her uncle, aged thirty-four

Charity Lashmore
née Bonny, his wife, aged thirty

Clara Lashmore
Emily's cousin, aged twelve

Martin Bonny
Emily's uncle

Woolton
a butler

Mrs Binns
a housekeeper

Bob
a footman

IN 1940

Oscar Fieldman
an air-raid warden

Minnie

Bill

George

Mrs Green

Mr Green

A Chauffeur

A Dance Band Vocalist

Nigel Chatterton-Brown

Clara Gilchrist
née Lashmore, aged sixty-six

Sir Lucas Lashmore
aged eighty-eight

IN 2010

Droid 1

Droid 2

Droid 3

Z1991 (Ziggi)
another droid

Char Tee (Charity)
aged twelve, Clara's great-great-grandchild

AT THE END OF TIME

Hoombean
a creature

The Time Keeper

Doubling

The minimum cast requirement for *Whenever* is nine (five male, four female) with the roles, it is suggested, allocated as follows:

WOMAN 1
Emily

WOMAN 2
Mrs Binns, Mrs Green, Guest at Party, The Time Keeper

WOMAN 3
Clara aged 12, Minnie, Guest at Party, Char Tee

WOMAN 4
Charity aged 30, Clara aged 66, Droid 1

MAN 1
Lucas aged 34, Lucas aged 88, Droid 2

MAN 2
Bob, George, Chauffeur, Vocalist/Guest at Party, Ziggi

MAN 3
Woolton, Mr Green, Guest at Party, Hoombean

MAN 4
Martin, Bill, Nigel Chatterton-Brown, Droid 3

MAN 5
Oscar

Songs

ACT ONE

Hiding
Emily, Clara

Time
Martin, Bob, Emily

Whenever
Emily

Wood for the Trees
Minnie, Oscar, Bill, George

Out of Sight
Band Vocalist

Deal
Lucas, Emily, Clare

Whenever (first reprise)
Emily, Oscar

ACT TWO

The Human Welcome Song
Droids

Communication
Char Tee, Emily, Oscar

A Joke's a Joke
Oscar

The End of Time
The Time Keeper

Whenever (second reprise)
Emily, Oscar, Ziggi

Whenever (third reprise)
Emily

WHENEVER

Act One

1886. In and around the Bonnys' large town house.

As the brief overture ends, a small area is lit to represent a cupboard under the stairs where Emily, aged nine, is hiding from her cousin Clara, aged twelve.

During the song, Emily runs from one hiding place to another, fleeing from the unseen Clara.

SONG: 'HIDING'

Emily (*in a breathless whisper*)
   I'm hiding
   From Cousin Clara.
   She mustn't find me,
   Please God, don't let her find me!
   This may seem like a children's game,
   I know it by another name
   Called torment –
   By Cousin Clara.

Clara (*taunting, calling*) Emily!

Emily
   Please save me,
   From Cousin Clara.
   She mustn't catch me,
   Dear Lord, don't let her catch me!
   Or she will torture me by turns
   With finger twists and chinese burns
   Inflicted
   By Cousin Clara.

Clara (*calling*) Emily!

Emily
Why she delights in doing this, I really cannot tell –
This twelve-year-old monstrosity, this relative from hell!

Somewhere from the darkness, Clara laughs.

I'm hunted
By cousin Clara.
She's sure to find me.

Clara
I'm close behind you!

Emily
I know, soon as she finds me,

Clara
There isn't a place that you can hide!

Emily
She's going to punish me for fun

Clara
How I enjoy this!

Emily
For little things I've never done.

Clara
Isn't this fun?

Emily
Inventions,

Clara
I hear you! I see you!

Emily
By cousin Clara.

Clara
You cannot escape from me –

Emily
Since she arrived to live with us, my so-called little friend,
I've knelt each bedtime praying for this horrid dream to end.

Clara
Emily!

Emily
She's nearer,
Vile cousin Clara!
Knows where I'm hiding –

Clara
Here I come!

Emily
Em'ly! Have to be brave now!

Clara
Frightened little girl!

Emily
I give my promise not to cry –

Clara
Cry, baby, cry!

Emily
It's all she wants, just let her try!

Clara
Her mama's not here . . .

Emily
I hate her!

Clara
Emily! Emily!

Emily
Foul cousin Clara!

Clara
Emily! Emily!

Emily
She's getting closer

Clara
Emily!

Emily
Closer –

Clara
Emily!

Emily
Closer –

Clara
Emily!

Emily
Closer.

Clara
Emily!

Clara catches Emily.

Emily Aaaaah!

Clara (*grasping both Emily's hands, triumphantly*) Got you!

Emily Ow!

Clara (*bending Emily's fingers*) Come along, say sorry. I'm sorry for hiding from you, Clara, come on. Kneel and say sorry. Say sorry, slave!

Clara forces Emily to her knees.

Emily (*trying not to react*) You're hurting!

Clara Then say sorry!

Emily No!

Clara You will be more sorry if you do not . . .

She gives Emily's fingers a sharp twist. Emily gives a long-drawn-out cry of pain. Clara releases her and steps back.

Mrs Binns (*off*) What is going on up there?

Clara (*in a whisper*) Now you are in trouble!

Mrs Binns, the housekeeper, hurries on angrily.

Mrs Binns What are you children up to? I have asked you a hundred times not to play outside your aunt's room while she is resting. You know she is unwell. Emily, was that you screaming and yelling again?

Emily I was –

Clara I told her, Mrs Binns, I said to her, Emily, Mrs Binns will be terribly cross if we play up here –

Mrs Binns Yes, Clara, that will do! (*gently, to Emily*) Now what was the noise for, Emily? Eh?

Emily I was – I was –

Clara She was being naughty, Mrs Binns.

Mrs Binns Clara, for the last time, I am talking to Emily! I want an answer, child. What made you scream this time?

Emily (*hesitantly*) I was – hiding . . . that's all.

Mrs Binns Hiding? Who from? Clara?

Clara We were playing hide-and-seek that's all, Mrs Binns. Emily screams because she's frightened of the dark.

Emily I do not!

Clara She thinks she sees monsters.

Emily I do not!

Mrs Binns Will you stop it this minute, both of you!

Charity, pale and tired, appears in the passageway. She is in her dressing gown and has evidently been disturbed.

Charity What is all this noise? What is the trouble, Mrs Binns?

Mrs Binns Oh, nothing, madam. Sorry to disturb you, Mrs Lashmore.

Charity Really, this is not good enough!

Clara Mama, Emily started playing out here after Mrs Binns had told her not to and I was trying to stop her but she wouldn't listen to me, Mama . . .

Emily I did not! I was only –

Charity Is this true, Mrs Binns? Have you been disobedient again, Emily?

Mrs Binns I am sorting it out, madam, I am just getting to the bottom of it –

Clara Mama, it is true! Emily just stood there and started screaming . . .

Emily No!

Charity You are a very naughty girl, Emily. I am unwell, you know that. I need my afternoon rest and now it has been utterly disturbed. I have this splitting headache as well . . .

Clara Oh, poor Mama . . .

Charity You are a thoughtless, inconsiderate child. Mrs Binns, you will take her to her room and lock the door. Emily is to have no supper tonight, do you hear?

Clara, behind Charity's back, gives a little dance of triumph.

Emily No!

Mrs Binns I think that is a trifle harsh, madam, if you don't mind my –

Charity This minute, Mrs Binns!

Emily (*simultaneously*) Why should I be locked in my room again?

Charity You will do as you're told, Emily!

Clara Emily, you're so naughty, really!

Emily (*collapsing in tears*) It is always my fault, it is so unfair!

Mrs Binns Emily, calm down now, calm down . . .

Woolton, the butler, enters.

Charity Emily! Emily! The girl is hysterical!

Emily I will not! I will not be sent to my room again!

Woolton Is there a problem, madam?

Emily I want to see Uncle Martin . . .

Charity Woolton, will you take this girl to her room instantly –

Woolton (*grabbing hold of Clara*) Certainly, madam.

Clara Ow!

Charity No, not that one, Woolton! The other one, you stupid man!

Woolton I beg your pardon, madam. Come along, Miss Emily.

Emily I need to see Uncle Martin.

Charity You cannot see your Uncle Martin. He is too busy with important work to waste time talking to hysterical children.

Clara Uncle Martin is going to make us all rich, isn't he, Mama?

Charity That will do, Clara.

Clara Papa says that, once the invention works properly, we will have all the money and all the power in the world. We will –

Charity (*very sharply*) Clara! Will you hold your tongue! I shall not tell you again. (*turning on Emily again*) Look at me, I'm shaking, I'm shaking all over now after this, you wicked little girl . . .

Clara Oh, Mama. Poor Mama . . .

Mrs Binns Let me help you back to your bed, madam . . .

Emily allows Woolton to take her hand.

Charity You are to lock that child in her room, Woolton. Her Uncle Lucas will determine her punishment when he returns from work. (*as she goes*) Look at the state of me now, look at the state of me . . .

Clara (*going with her*) Poor Mama. Poor Mama.

Charity goes off assisted by Mrs Binns and Clara. Woolton sighs.

Emily (*more muted*) It was not my fault, Woolton. I promise it was not.

Woolton Alas, in this household, when it comes to apportioning blame, miss, there appears neither rhyme nor reason. Please, come along.

Emily (*as they move*) Woolton, is my uncle at home?

Woolton Your Uncle Lucas, miss?

Emily No, of course not Uncle Lucas. Uncle Martin . . .

Woolton Ah, Mr Bonny. I believe so, miss. Shut away in his workshop, as usual, all day and most of the night.

Emily I need to see him now.

Woolton Miss Emily, you heard your aunt . . .

Emily Please. For one minute. Aunt Charity would never know . . .

Woolton I could be dismissed from my post, Miss Emily.

Emily They would not dare. They could never manage without you, Woolton.

Woolton Oh, no one is irreplaceable, Miss Emily.

Emily Please, Woolton.

Woolton (*reluctantly*) Oh, dear. One minute, then.

Emily Thank you! Thank you! Thank you!

Woolton I am getting soft. I've always given in to you ever since you arrived, ever since you were four years old.

Emily Oh, Woolton, this was such a happy place before they all came to live here. Before Uncle Lucas and Aunt Charity and Clara . . .

Woolton I think, as you grew up, living here alone with your Uncle Martin was considered inappropriate, Miss Emily.

Emily What does inappropriate mean?

Woolton Er – I will explain that to you when you have grown up even more, miss.

Emily But I was not living here alone with Uncle Martin. You and Mrs Binns and Cook and Bob were here, too.

Woolton I am afraid in polite society, miss, people like us do not officially exist.

Emily You do to me. You are the most important people in the whole world as far as I am concerned.

They have reached the top of the staircase.

Woolton Thank you, miss. Here we are. Now, I have your promise, remember?

Emily One minute. I promise.

Emily starts to descend the staircase. We follow her into the cellar which serves as Martin's workshop. It consists of a workbench upon which is a seemingly aimless jumble of wires and primitive electronic equipment, the control unit for Martin's Time Machine. Separate is the Machine itself, though it is scarcely recognisable as such, simply a circle marked on the floor with, hanging directly above it, a dome filled with wires and lights.

Martin is making adjustments to the control unit on the workbench. Watching him is Bob, a footman, pressed into service as a lab assistant.

Martin (*his head buried amidst the wiring*) Ah . . . I think I've found our problem, Bob . . . we have a naughty little rogue here who has disconnected himself . . . there we are . . . aha! . . . contact is resumed . . . Now . . . (*emerging and seeing Emily*) What are you doing down here, young woman? I've given strict instru – (*realising who it is*) Ah! It's Emily! Emily-Emily-Emily. My dear child, how nice to see you.

Emily Hello, Uncle Martin.

Martin Bob, look who's here. It's Emily.

Bob 'Ullo, Miss Emily.

Emily Hello, Bob. Uncle, I need to speak with you . . .

Martin Yes, of course. (*proffering a paper bag*) Can I tempt you to a mint humbug?

Emily No, thank you. Uncle, I –

Martin Great aid to concentration, humbugs. I swear by them. Dear old Bob here, Emily, he's helping me with my experiments, aren't you, Bob?

Bob That's right, sir.

Martin Patience of a saint has Bob. He sits around for hours waiting for me. I've had him testing hot-air balloons, standing in tanks of water in home-made diving suits, trying out an electric bicycle. I've even fired him out of a cannon, poor chap – remember the cannon, Bob?

Bob (*cheerfully*) Oh, I remember the cannon, sir.

Martin Bang! Went for miles, didn't you? (*He roars with laughter.*)

Bob Four hundred and seventy-four yards, two feet, eight inches, sir.

Martin Broke your arm, didn't you? What else?

Bob (*cheerfully*) Left arm, right collarbone, both wrists and a multiple fracture of the left leg, sir.

Martin Now, that's what I call travelling, Bob. They can keep their new-fangled steam engines. Mark my words, Emily, in twenty-five years everyone will be travelling by cannon.

Emily Uncle, may I speak with you for a minute?

Martin (*oblivious*) That's the future, Emily. The future is in cannons, eh, Bob? What it must have felt like, flying through the air at sixty feet per second!

Bob Very 'xilarating, sir.

Martin Exhilarating, yes. Good word, Bob!

Bob Till I landed, of course.

Martin Don't you worry, we'll sort that out, we'll sort the landing bit out. There are always little drawbacks to start with, Bob.

Emily Uncle, I must speak to you. It's very important . . .

Martin Emily, you are just in time to see Bob off on another remarkable journey. What we have here is the prototype Temporal Displacement Vehicle. Or to put it in common parlance, a Time Machine. Do you know what I mean by a Time Machine?

Emily I have never heard of one before, Uncle.

Martin That's because nobody's invented one before. It is a machine that will enable us to travel through time. Imagine that. Travelling back to the Roman Colosseum, Cleopatra on the Nile, the England of Shakespeare . . .

Emily If I could go back two years, that is all I would ever want.

Martin But, Emily, most thrilling of all – this machine is capable of travelling forward to the future, Emily! For the first time mankind will be able to see into the future. Think of it – if we don't like what we see, we can come back and change it. No more wars, no more suffering! We will foresee and therefore anticipate, Emily! We will be able to alter events for the good of all mankind.

Emily But will it work, Uncle? One or two of your inventions have –

Martin Oh! Emily, they should have christened you Thomas. Doubting Thomas. Admittedly, we are having – teething problems – we are not yet able to make it travel backwards but – minor details! See for yourself. Bob, dear chap, be so good as to step onto the Portal. Let's give Emily a demonstration.

Bob Certainly, sir.

Martin One can control the machine from on board the Portal. But in this case I shall direct things myself from this master console. Dear old Bob, he's quite hopeless, poor chap, when it comes to moving knobs and levers. I'm going to send you two minutes into the future this time, Bob.

Bob Two minutes. Very good, sir.

Martin Don't forget your clock!

Bob Oh no, don't forget me clock!

Bob picks up a large mantel clock and steps back into the centre of the portal. Music under.

Emily Why does he need a clock, Uncle?

Martin (*to Emily*) Ah, most important, Emily. Bob will use the clock to measure elapsed time during his journey. For him that should, theoretically, hardly be measurable – a mere twinkling of an eye – whereas for us – in real time – a full two minutes should pass. Now, Bob, remember to take note of every sensation, every feeling you experience. The scientific way, Bob. What is the time by your clock now?

Bob Exactly twenty past, sir.

Martin (*looking at his pocket watch*) Twenty past. Very good. I will see you at twenty-two minutes past the hour. My time. *Bon voyage*, Bob!

Bob Thank you very much, sir. And the same to you.

Emily (*anxiously*) Will he be alright, Uncle?

Martin Good heavens, of course he will! Bob has a charmed life. Ready?

Bob Ready, sir!

Martin Go!

SONG: 'TIME' (PART ONE)

Martin, as he sings, excitedly fiddles with levers. A circular, transparent wall rises up out of the floor and surrounds Bob. It begins to fill with smoke as lights flash from the dome above. Bob, still clutching the clock, is obscured from view.

Martin
  Set the condenser
  Then load the dispenser,
  The temporal sensor
  Just slightly intenser . . .
  Now check the transformer . . .

Bob
  It's getting much warmer . . .

Martin
  If all this works it will be quite sublime.
  Ease the inducer –
  That feels a bit looser –
  The next bit is easy.

Bob
  I feels a bit queasy –

Martin
  Tune up the traction,
  We're all set for action –

Bob
>I hope I don't end up before my time.

Martin
>It's all aboard for a journey in the Time Machine.
>If you're early we'll see you later.
>Yes, it's a voyage of a lifetime that you've not yet seen –
>You'll be back here before you leave.
>Checking the lighting –

The lights all flash briefly.

Emily
>Oh! That bit's exciting!

Martin
>The signal's receiving –

Bob
>It's time I'm leaving!

Martin
>Adjust alternator –

Bob
>I'll see you a bit later!

Martin
>What joy to watch those needles start to climb!
>Feel a vibration?

Bob (*vibrating madly*)
>Well, just a sensation –

Martin
>We're on to a winner!

Bob
>I'm losing me dinner . . .

Martin
>Witness the light show!

Emily
   Will he be alright, though?

Bob
   I hope I'm not cut off before my prime!
   'Cos here I am on a journey in the Time Machine.
   If I'm early you'll see me later.
   Yes, it's a voyage of a lifetime that I've not yet seen –
   I'll be back here before I leave.

All
   So all aboard for a journey in the Time Machine.
   If you're early we'll see you later.
   Yes, it's a voyage of a lifetime that you've not yet seen –
   You'll be back here before you leave.

A great mechanical whirring and grinding builds to a climax. The wall sinks back into the floor. Bob is no longer there. The song ends.

Martin Bob has now travelled, Emily, two minutes into our future. Hopefully.

Emily If it works, it will make us very rich, won't it, Uncle?

Martin Possibly, possibly.

Emily There is nothing we will not be able to achieve. All the money we want –

Martin Oh, no, no, no . . .

Emily All the power that we want . . .

Martin Certainly not, Emily. It cannot be used for personal gain. I'm surprised at you. Who has been filling your head with this nonsense?

Emily Apparently that was what Uncle Lucas was saying.

Martin (*frowning*) Then, Lucas is very much mistaken. I shall tell him so the next time I see him. (*consulting his watch*) I hope Bob's alright . . .

Emily Uncle, I know how important your work is and it is very wrong of me to disturb you but you are the only one who can help me, you see . . .

Martin is busy at his bench. From the top of the staircase, Woolton's voice is heard.

Woolton (*off*) Miss Emily!

Emily It's Aunt Charity and Uncle Lucas. I believe that they hate me.

Martin Hate you?

Emily I am unable to do anything right for them. Everything I do, they criticise.

Martin Where on earth did you get this absurd notion, child?

Woolton (*off*) Miss Emily! You've had more than a minute, miss.

Emily (*calling*) Yes, I'm coming, Woolton, I promise! Uncle, they never –

Martin Emily, both Lucas and Charity are extremely fond of you. Why, Charity was saying to me the other day what a sweet-natured child you were.

Emily Oh, she may say that to you! But the moment your back is turned –

Martin I invited them to live here, Emily, because I felt you would be less lonely. Admittedly, Lucas had some financial problems but really it was for your sake, child. And their daughter Clara being about the same age – I thought she would be company for you –

Emily Clara? Clara is worst of all. She delights in bullying me. I have tried to be her friend, I swear, but she turns me away.

Woolton (*off*) Miss Emily, you promised . . .

Emily Yes, Woolton, I'm coming. (*starting up the staircase*) Please speak to them. Please, if you love me at all, Uncle.

Martin Emily, I will certainly not see you unhappy. But I'm sure it's all in your imagination. I'm sure it's – (*suddenly distracted*) Oh, dear!

Emily What is it?

Martin Where's Bob? Bob should have returned by now. No! Listen! Listen!

The same mechanical whirring and grinding as before. The wall starts to rise from the floor. Bob stands as before, still clutching his clock.

Martin Bob! How was it? How was it, dear fellow?

SONG: 'TIME' (PART TWO)

Bob
First I was sinking,
My eyes they were blinking,
Them lights started winking
And I got to thinking . . .

Martin
. . . But what did you see there . . . ?

Bob
. . . I'm a loony to be there . . .

Martin
My boy, you've just achieved a British first . . .

Emily
    What did it feel like?

Bob
    Well slightly unreal, like . . .
    My heart it was pumpin',
    Both legs started jumpin' –

Martin
    Did you observe, though?

Bob
    I did feel my nerve go.
    I held my breath until I thought I'd burst!
    'Cos there I was on a journey in the Time Machine.
    If I'm early please see me later.
    Yes, it's a voyage of a lifetime and I've turned bright green –
    Get me back here before I leave.

Martin
    Hard to believe it . . .

Emily
    . . . you'd ever achieve it?

Martin
    Report your sensations?

Emily
    Oh! Congratulations!

Martin
    Answer my question . . .

Bob
    I've mild indigestion,
    My nervous state could prob'bly be improved . . .

Martin (*taking Bob's clock to the bench*)
    Check what's elapsed when . . .

Bob
   I think I've collapsed, then . . . (*He drops to the floor.*)

Emily (*alarmed*)
   Oh, he's getting weaker!

Martin (*unaware*)
   Aha! Eureka!

Emily
   He needs attention!

Martin
   Beyond comprehension!
   The hands on Bob's own clock have barely moved!
   So all aboard for a journey in the Time Machine.
   If you're early we'll see you later.
   Yes, it's a voyage of a lifetime that you've not yet
      seen –
   You'll be back here before you leave.

All
   So all aboard for a journey in the Time Machine.
   If you're early we'll see you later.
   Yes, it's a voyage of a lifetime that you've not yet
      seen –
   You'll be back here before you leave.

By the end of the song, we have cross-faded to Emily's bedroom. Emily unhappily sits on the bed. Woolton stands in the doorway.

Emily Woolton!

Woolton Yes, miss?

Emily Will you bring me a lamp before it grows dark? Please don't leave me in the dark.

Woolton Don't worry, miss, someone will bring you a lamp, I promise. I must lock this door now, miss. Your Aunt Charity's orders.

Emily (*bravely*) Very well.

Woolton is about to depart. A tall, dark figure appears in the doorway behind him.

Emily (*rising, startled*) Uncle Lucas . . .

Lucas Very well, Woolton. You may leave the door.

Woolton I can assure you, sir, Miss Emily has really not –

Lucas That will be all, Woolton.

Woolton Very good, Mr Lashmore.

Woolton leaves. Lucas studies Emily for a second or two.

Lucas So, young lady. Your Aunt Charity tells me you have been misbehaving yet again. Is this true?

Emily No, Uncle.

Lucas You were not misbehaving?

Emily No. I was –

Lucas Are you implying, then, that my wife is a liar?

Emily No, Uncle.

Lucas She is not a liar?

Emily No, Uncle.

Lucas Then she is telling the truth?

Emily Yes. I mean –

Lucas Then you were misbehaving?

Emily No. I was not, I was –

Lucas (*sharply*) Do not equivocate with me, young woman. Either you were misbehaving or you were not. Which is it to be?

Emily shakes her head, trapped by the logic of all this.

From your silence, I deduce consent. In truth, Emily, it was you and not my wife who was lying? You *were* misbehaving?

Emily (*defeated, softly*) If my aunt says so –

Lucas She does indeed say so. This is by no means the first time, is it, Emily? I have been patient with you, young lady, for far too long. Over the past months, I have tried encouragement, I have tried inducement, I have even been reduced to threats, which you should know is totally alien to my nature. However, it seems nothing we have tried, your aunt and I, has done anything to correct your wicked, sinful ways. It seems I am now driven to sterner measures. Do you understand what I mean by that, Emily?

Emily (*quietly*) You cannot do that . . .

Lucas What? What did you say?

Emily You cannot do that. Uncle Martin would not allow it.

Lucas Indeed? We shall see what I may or may not do in my own house.

Emily This is not your house, it is my house. It belonged to my parents. When they were – when they died – they left it to me. This is my house . . .

Lucas Oh, no, no, no . . .

Emily They did! They left it to me! Uncle Martin told me –

Lucas No, Emily. When your parents died in that unfortunate accident, they left it in what is known as a trust. Of which the trustees are your Aunt Charity, your Uncle Martin and myself, all of us pledged to look after and maintain this property until such time as you come of age. Now, Emily, I need hardly remind you that you do not come of age for another twelve years. Which may seem in the scheme of things very little time at all, but I can promise you, if your unruly behaviour continues, as far as you are concerned it could well seem an eternal lifetime. So we will see what I can or cannot do, will we not?

Emily Uncle Martin will not allow you to hit me.

Lucas Martin? Your Uncle Martin is far too busy to be bothered with you –

During the next, Clara enters with an oil lamp.

Emily I have just told Uncle what has been happening. If necessary, I shall ask him to throw you all out of this house.

Lucas Indeed?

Emily All of you – (*to Clara*) including you!

Lucas Ah, Clara, my dear. Good girl, you have brought our miscreant a lamp, have you? Something to lighten her gloom? Though I doubt whether it will be sufficient to illuminate her dark little soul, alas.

Clara giggles sycophantically.

Do we say thank you to Clara, Emily? I think we do. If we wish to keep our lamp. What do you say?

Emily (*in a whisper*) Thank you, Clara.

Lucas (*going*) I shall be back, young woman. Then we shall have a reckoning, you and I, never fear. Clara, be sure to lock the door when you leave.

Clara Yes, Papa.

Lucas goes.

(*gleefully*) I was listening at the door. You are going to be beaten. And I am glad you are. I hope you cry and cry. You deserve it, you little liar.

Emily (*trying to remain calm*) Please leave my room, at once!

Clara Like a horse in the street! Like a common servant girl!

Emily Get out!

Clara Think about that. Just think about it. Better still, think about it in the dark!

Spitefully, Clara blows out the lamp. The room is now very dark.

Emily (*alarmed*) Clara!

Clara (*laughing*) Sleep well!

Emily (*calling after her*) Clara! Do not leave me in the dark! Please! You cannot leave me in the dark!

Clara has gone. We hear the door slam and the sound of the key in the lock. There is a small pool of light on the bed from the window.

(*weakly*) Clara!

Silence. Emily sits on the bed.

SONG: 'WHENEVER'

Whenever I'm afraid,
When I'm alone,
With not a soul to guide me,
To see me through the night
And whisper everything's all right –

Although there's no special place can hide me
From all the fear of the dark inside me –

It won't seem long till everything
Becomes as bright as day.
I know the sun will rise,
That come the dawn
I tell myself, as sure as day breaks,
I will laugh away my fears –
Whenever I'm afraid.

The song ends but the music continues, growing slowly more sinister as her door is unlocked and creaks open. Nervously, Emily goes to investigate. She pulls open the door and creeps along the dark passageway. Music reflects Emily's increasing apprehension.

It stops abruptly as someone in the darkness taps her on the shoulder. It is Bob.

Emily (*with a half scream*) Bob! What are you doing?

Bob Sorry, Miss Emily.

Emily What are you doing here?

Bob (*all in a breath*) Your uncle, Mr Martin, sent me out to get some more humbugs 'cos he run out of humbugs and I buyed the humbugs and I comes back with the humbugs only by then Mr Lucas he's down there as well and they're like talking angry like, so I still got the humbugs.

Emily (*barely following this*) Mr Lucas and Mr Martin were arguing?

Bob Shoutin' and yellin' and threatenin'.

Emily Where's Mr Woolton? Have you summoned him?

Bob He's gone, miss, Mr Woolton. Mr Lucas, he dismissed him for disobeying . . . He's packed 'em both off. Mr Woolton and Mrs Binns.

Emily Mrs Binns as well?

Bob She were the one told me to unlock your door 'fore she left. I put 'em both in a cab for the railway station. All their bags and baggage. They've both gone to stay with her sister in Hartypool. Just temporary, like. Till they're newly repositioned, like . . .

They reach the top of the spiral staircase. Sounds of raised voices from below.

Lucas (*off, angrily*) . . . if anyone is living in cloud-cuckoo land it is you, Martin. You have a discovery worth millions of pounds and like the idiot you are you are prepared to throw it all away . . .

Bob (*over this*) Listen! They're still at it, d'you hear?

Emily (*over this and the next*) We have to stop them. What are we to do?

Bob We?

Emily It sounds as if they are about to come to blows. We must send for someone.

Bob Who?

Emily I don't know. A policeman?

Bob A policeman!

Emily Unless you prefer to go down there yourself . . .

Bob (*handing her the bag of humbugs*) Here! I'll go and fetch a policeman!

Emily Bob! Bob! Oh, heavens!

Bob has gone. Emily hesitates, then, rather cautiously, starts to edge her way down the spiral staircase. Eventually, she is in the room and Lucas and Martin have appeared, though they are too absorbed with their quarrel to notice her.

Martin (*continuing during the last*) . . . unlike the profiteering rogue who's prepared to exploit everyone he meets purely for his own personal gain. I'm telling you, Lucas, finally and for all I refuse to become part of your squalid, profiteering little schemes! Now get out of my workshop, at once, do you hear me?

Lucas Workshop? You call this a workshop? A damp, ill-equipped little cellar run by a half-baked idealist with a half-witted assistant! And now, for once, you have stumbled upon something that can change our lives forever and what do you do? You turn your back on it!

Martin Because if I took that course I can see precisely where that path would lead, Lucas. Directly to men like you. Unprincipled scoundrels who are prepared to go to any lengths to line their own pockets. No matter whom they may ruin, whom they may destroy in the process . . .

Lucas Do not start preaching to me, Martin, with your half-baked idealism!

Emily has reached the bottom of the stairs. She draws away to a corner of the room too terrified to speak.

Martin . . . you have always been the same, Lucas, ever since I have known you. A selfish, unscrupulous, immoral –

Lucas If you are referring to the fact that I am the only one in this miserable family with any scrap of business sense . . .

Martin Business sense? Business sense? You are an out-and-out crook, Lucas! You tricked my half-witted sister into marrying you – and now you are trying to steal other people's ideas and pass them off as your own!

Lucas Let me tell you, Martin, if it had not been for me this family would all be in the gutter . . .

Martin It was a perfectly happy family until you wormed your way into it . . . you miserable conniving trickster. You have spent your way through that wretched woman's fortune and now you're proposing to start on mine. You are a trickster and a crook!

Lucas (*livid*) Don't you call me that! How dare you call me that!

Martin What is the matter? Too close to the truth, is it?

Martin turns his back on Lucas and makes to move away to the further part of the room.

Trickster! Trickster! Trickster!

Lucas snatches up a knife from the workbench.

Lucas (*infuriated*) I am warning you, Martin!

Martin (*going*) Trickster!

Martin goes out of sight. Lucas gives a roar of rage and chases after him. Sounds of a struggle, then a final cry. Emily stands frozen with fear. A silence.

Emily (*at last, nervously*) Uncle Martin! (*She listens.*) Uncle Martin?

The sound of slow footsteps from the darkest corner of the cellar. Emily strains to make out who it is. Lucas steps from the shadows. His clothing is bloody. He stares at her.

Lucas Don't be alarmed, Emily.

Emily (*in a horrified whisper*) What have you done? Is Uncle Martin . . . ?

Lucas (*starting to advance on her*) There has been an accident, Emily, but there is no need to be frightened.

Emily (*retreating, horrified*) You – have killed him.

Lucas (*softly still*) Come here. Don't run away from me. Come here, I say!

Emily (*calling*) Bob! Bob! Aunt Charity! Clara!

Lucas Clara, like the good child she is, is reading to your aunt in her bedroom. They will never hear you. Come here!

Emily (*still retreating*) Keep away!

Lucas You do not wish to see me angry, do you now? Come here, Emily!

Emily (*retreating around the workbench*) Keep away from me!

Lucas (*losing patience, suddenly violently lunging at her*) I said come here!

As he grabs for her, he knocks a lever on the bench. The Time Machine starts to power up. Lucas grabs at Emily again and holds her briefly. Emily twists free and runs for the Time Machine. The wall is just starting to rise from the floor. Emily jumps in. Lucas, too late, tries to stop the Machine using the workbench controls. Seeing this is not working, he runs to the Machine but can only walk round the outside, shouting at Emily through the wall.

You cannot hide in there for ever, Emily. I can wait. I have all the time in the world, my dear.

Emily scrabbles feverishly with the control buttons inside the Portal.

Emily (*during the last*) How does it work? I have to make it work. I have to!

Lucas (*banging the side of the machine*) Emily! Come out of there, this instant!

Emily finally gets the Machine to operate. The wall fills with mist, as before, and the whirring, grinding sound is heard. The canopy lights start to flash. Lucas rushes back to the workbench and feverishly tries to stop her.

(*stabbing vainly at the controls*) Come back! Come back! Wretched machine!

He smashes part of the workbench but the Machine still gathers impetus.

I will be waiting. You cannot escape me, Emily. Wherever you go – wherever you are – I'll be waiting for you – whenever you are! Whenever! Whenever!

His voice is drowned out by the Machine. This time, though, the Machine remains whilst the surroundings grow dark and the basement goes. The Machine continues for a few more seconds and then comes to a halt. The wall descends into the floor and we see Emily, dazed and a little shaken.
   Silence.

Emily (*looking around her, softly*) Where am I? Where is this? *When* is this?

At first, the surrounding area is in darkness, as if Emily's eyes are not accustomed to the gloom. Echoing in the distance, we hear the sound of a radio playing a thirties dance-music version of 'Out of Sight'.

What is that extraordinary noise?

She moves cautiously towards the sound. As she passes through a doorway, the lights come up to reveal a platform in a London tube station during an air raid. It is 1940. There are several huddled figures, some sitting, some lying on makeshift beds. Overhead, the sound of ack-ack guns and the occasional distant explosion. Emily stands terrified. Music under.

(*in a whisper*) Where am I? What is this place?

A louder, closer bang. Emily cowers.

Minnie It's alright, you're safe down here. Don't be frightened, dearie.

Bill You're alright down the underground here, sweetheart, the bombs can't get you down here, see?

Emily Bombs?

Another bang. Emily cowers.

George Busy tonight, eh?

Minnie Yes, he's busy tonight is Mr Hitler.

Bill Little blighter.

Minnie Blighter! Don't worry, they can't get you down here, dearie . . .

George Not yet, anyway.

Minnie What you mean, George, not yet?

George I heard the Germans were working on a bomb that would chase yer. Wherever you went it would chase yer, till it found yer and then – boom – Gawd help yer.

Minnie What's he talking about?

Bill Look, just shut up, George, alright? You can see the kiddie's scared enough.

Another louder explosion.

Emily (*flinching, in a whisper*) I've died and gone to hell.

Minnie Ah! Look, bless her, she's terrified . . .

Oscar, an ARP warden, enters hurriedly.

Bill What's it like up there, Oscar? That last one sounded close.

Oscar Methodist church on the corner . . .

Minnie Oh, no . . . Badly damaged?

Oscar Pile of rubble. Rubble. Cheer up!

Minnie Oh, dear . . .

George They're bombing churches now. It'll be schools next. And orphanages. They'll be going after orphanages, you mark my words.

Minnie Don't say that, George, you'll frighten her again! Oscar, can you talk to that little kiddie? She's terrified.

Oscar (*seeing Emily for the first time*) Well, stripe me pink! Hello, young 'un, where did you spring from, eh? Cheer up!

Minnie Look, she's all dressed up in her little dress, look. See? She must have been going to a party. You going to a party, dearie, were you? Yes! She were going to a party, I bet.

Oscar (*moving closer to Emily, kindly*) Where's your mum and dad then, love? They down here with you, are they?

Emily shrinks from him but doesn't reply.

Minnie Lovely hair, hasn't she? Look at her little hair.

Oscar Come on, you can talk to me. Cheer up! Where do you live, then?

Minnie I used to have hair like that before the war.

Oscar Minnie, just a tick, I'm trying to talk to the kiddie. What's your name, eh?

Emily (*softly*) Emily.

Minnie Aaah! (*to the others*) Emily.

Oscar That's a pretty name, isn't it? I used to have an auntie called Emily.

Minnie Aaah! Oscar used to have an auntie called Emily.

Oscar Now, where's your mum and dad, love?

Emily They're – they're . . .

Oscar Yes? Where? They're where?

Emily They're dead.

Oscar Dead?

Minnie (*to the others*) Dead.

Emily In a – in an accident . . .

Oscar Accident. Oh, dear.

Minnie Air raid, most like.

Oscar In an air raid was it, love?

Emily No. The coach turned over.

Oscar Coach? You mean a motor coach? Railway coach?

Emily No. The horses bolted and the coach turned over.

Oscar Oh. Fancy that. Never mind, cheer up!

Minnie You wouldn't catch me on a horse. Not with a war on.

Another loud bang. Emily jumps.

George All be over soon. They'll be invading, any day now. There'll be stormtroopers storming up through Kent . . .

Minnie Oh, do be quiet, George.

George Pillagin' and lootin' and . . . worse.

Oscar That's enough of that!

Emily (*finding her voice at last*) My uncle has just killed my uncle, you see . . .

Bill She's what?

Oscar (*to the others*) Her uncle's just killed her uncle.

Minnie Her uncle's just killed her uncle?

Oscar That's what she says.

George You mean he killed himself? He committed suicide?

Emily No, no! My Uncle Lucas killed my Uncle Martin . . .

Oscar Your Uncle Lucas killed your Uncle Martin?

Emily And then Uncle Lucas tried to kill me.

Oscar Then your Uncle Lucas tried to kill you?

Minnie Why did he want to do that, dearie?

Emily (*increasingly agitated*) Because I'd seen him kill my Uncle Martin, of course!

George I had a dog called Lucas.

Oscar And what happened, then, love?

George He was run over by a rubbish cart.

Emily (*in a rush*) I tried to call for help only Aunt Charity and Cousin Clara were both upstairs and Uncle Lucas had already dismissed Woolton and Mrs Binns and Bob ran off to find a policeman, so I hid aboard the Time Machine that Uncle Martin had been making with Bob and I set it going and before I knew it I found myself here. You see?

Pause. They all stare at her. Oscar leads them all in brief applause. Music under.

Oscar Very good. Well done. You make that up yourself, love, did you?

Emily I'm not making it up . . .

Minnie Was that your party piece? Very good. I should just try and speak a bit slower next time, dearie.

Emily (*moving to the door*) It's true! It's true! (*looking at them*) Believe me! Come along then. I will show you! I will show you the Machine!

Oscar Oy! Where you going, love? You can't go that way.

Emily This is the way I came.

Oscar That's an emergency exit. Only for emergencies. You can't go that way.

Emily This is where I came from! My machine is in there!

Minnie She's very well spoken, isn't she?

Emily (*shouting at them*) Why will none of you believe me? What are you all doing here in my cellar, anyway?

Oscar Come on, come on! Calm down, now. Calm down! Cheer up! Tell you what, how about this? You know this one, don't you? You must do.

SONG: 'WOOD FOR THE TREES'

Oscar
 Don't you ever let a ratter eat his dinner off your
  platter

Bill
 It will only make him fatter when he's eaten all your
  batter

Oscar
> And he'll simply want a natter but his talkin' doesn't matter

Bill
> If the constant chitter-chatter makes you madder than a hatter

Emily (*speaking, in frustration*) Oh, heavens above!

All
> Before you go climbing the mulberry bush
> Make sure there's a favourable breeze.
> You'd better not stop till you get to the top
> Or you won't see the wood for the trees.

Emily (*speaking*) If you would just let me show you –

Minnie
> If a lovely lady potter throws her clay upon your blotter
> It is better if you spot her that you rapidly forgot her.
> Just imagine if her otter marks your carpet with his trotter
> You will only feel a rotter if you got your gun and shot her.

Emily (*speaking*) You're all completely mad!

All
> Before you go climbing the mulberry bush
> Make sure there's a favourable breeze.
> You'd better not stop till you get to the top
> Or you won't see the wood for the trees.

Emily (*speaking*) All I need to do is to –

George
> If you stand out in the gutter and you spread yourself with butter
> You will hear the people mutter that you're certainly a nutter,

And no matter how you stutter that it's good to have
   a flutter,
They will only shout and splutter that you should have
   closed the shutter

All
   Before you go climbing the mulberry bush
   Make sure there's a favourable breeze.
   You'd better not stop till you get to the top
   Or you won't see the wood for the trees.
   Before you go climbing the mulberry bush
   Make sure there's a favourable breeze.
   You'd better not stop till you get to the top
   Or you won't see the wood –
   No reason you should –
   You won't see the wood for the trees!

Towards the end, the group is joined by Mrs Green. She stares intently at Emily, consulting an old faded Victorian photograph. As the song finishes amidst great merriment, the all-clear siren is heard.

Oscar (*officially*) There's the all-clear! (*calling*) All-clear, now!

Mrs Green darts forward and smothers the startled Emily in a close embrace.

Mrs Green (*overjoyed*) Oh, my darling! Here you are! We've been so worried. Dear God, we thought we'd lost you!

Oscar Is she with you then?

Mrs Green Her father and I have been worried to death. How could you do this to us, running off without a word?

Emily (*extricating her head for a second*) What are you doing? I'm not –

Mrs Green pulls Emily tightly to her again. Emily makes indignant muffled sounds from the recesses of Mrs Green.

Mrs Green Come along home at once, you silly, silly girl.

Oscar You're her mother, then?

Mrs Green (*squeezing Emily, fondly*) Yes, of course, I'm her mother!

More sounds from Emily.

Minnie She just told us her parents were dead.

Mrs Green (*laughing*) Oh, really. Emily! You naughty girl!

Mrs Green holds Emily's head, squeezing both her cheeks with her fingers and thumbs so that all Emily can produce is gurgling sounds.

Why do you make up these tales? She has this wild imagination.

Minnie Naughty girl. An only, is she?

Mrs Green (*drawing Emily to her again*) Yes, our one and only.

Minnie Pride and joy! That'd explain it! Naughty girl!

George I was one of twelve.

Emily (*briefly free again*) I've never seen you before in my – mmmmppph! (*She is swiftly smothered again.*)

Mrs Green Come along, darling. Let's go and find Daddy and we'll take you home! Thank you so much for looking after her, all of you.

Minnie Pleasure, dear! Any time!

Emily is borne away by Mrs Green. She struggles and manages the occasional word but is promptly silenced again. They look on amused. Only Oscar seems troubled.

Bill (*shaking his head, amused*) Kids these days!

Minnie I don't know, I'm sure!

George Out of control, in my opinion.

Bill Well, see you in the morning then.

George If there is a morning.

Minnie What do you mean by that?

Bill Take no notice of him.

George I've heard there could be German troops everywhere by dawn . . .

Minnie How do you know?

Bill He's a fifth columnist, that's why. 'Night, Oscar!

George What are you talking about? I'm no spy.

Minnie Wouldn't be surprised if you were. They're everywhere, these days, aren't they? 'Night, Oscar!

George Don't start calling me a spy. Careless talk costs lives, mate! 'Night!

They have all gone except Oscar.

Oscar (*abstracted*) 'Night. (*to himself*) Why didn't her mother have a wedding ring, then? (*He comes to a decision.*) Charlie!

Charlie (*off*) Hello?

Oscar Can you see to things here? Check the blackout? I got to do something.

Charlie (*off*) Righty-o.

Oscar goes. The scene changes to the street. Mrs Green comes on, dragging Emily.

Emily Where are you taking me? Who are you?

Mrs Green Listen, shut up will you, you wretched brat? Shut up, do you hear?

Mr Green appears.

Mr Green What's going on? What's happening?

Mrs Green Oh, there you are!

Mr Green Is that her? Don't tell me that's her!

Mrs Green What's it look like? Where the hell have you been?

Mr Green I told you, I had a business meeting.

Mrs Green With that barmaid, I bet? Good job one of us was here. We'd have been in right trouble otherwise. Look, give me a hand with her, will you? She's a right little vixen. She's bitten me twice . . .

Together they grab Emily.

Emily Let go of me!

Mr Green (*as they struggle*) Is this really her?

Mrs Green Got to be, look how she's dressed. Ow!

Mr Green Can't believe it after all these years. (*to Emily*) Listen, you try biting me, I'll knock your teeth out, alright?

Mrs Green Where the hell's the car gone to? What a night!

Mr Green He's probably still in a shelter somewhere. How many years have we been waiting for her?

Mrs Green God knows. Who cares? We're getting paid, aren't we? Ah, there he is.

The Chauffeur enters.

Chauffeur Big bomb crater in the road there. I had to come the other way.

Mrs Green Alright, let's get her in the car, then.

Chauffeur Blimey, is that her? At last!

Mrs Green Quickly! For God's sake! Don't stand around here!

They bundle Emily into the back seat between Mr and Mrs Green, the Chauffeur in front.

Emily Where are we going? Where are you taking me?

Mrs Green You'll find out. All in good time.

Emily (*looking around her*) What is this thing? Where are the horses?

Mrs Green It's a motor car, dear. Have you never been in a motor car before?

Emily No.

Mrs Green Well, you're in for a treat then, aren't you? Sit back and enjoy the ride.

The engine roars as the Chauffeur jams the car into gear and they set off.

Emily (*alarmed*) Oh, heavens above!

Mr Green Keep still!

Emily We're going too fast! Slow down, please slow down!

Chauffeur I'm only going twenty-five.

Emily (*screaming*) Please!

The car turns a corner or two. Emily shrieks each time and covers her eyes.

Chauffeur Can't you keep her quiet? It's very hard to drive, you know.

Mr Green Listen, if you don't belt up, kid, I'm going to stop this car and stuff you in the boot, alright?

Emily Stuff me in your what?

Mr Green The boot. Now shut it!

Emily You can't put me in your boots. I would not fit in your boots, you must not put me in your boots, please!

Mrs Green Leave the kid alone, Alf! Alright.

Emily He is going to stuff me in his boots!

Mrs Green No, he's not. Now quieten down.

Emily (*calmer*) Where are you taking me?

Mrs Green To see an old friend of yours. Mrs Gilchrist.

Emily Mrs Gilchrist? I do not know any Mrs Gilchrist!

Mrs Green Oh, I think you do, dear. She certainly knows you.

The car pulls up sharply, causing Emily to react again.

Chauffeur Here we are. I hope you don't want me to take her anywhere else. I need a lie down after that.

Mrs Green No, we won't be needing you again, Sandy. You can put the car away. Emily's – not going anywhere else. (*to Emily*) Come on, come and say hello to Mrs Gilchrist.

Mr and Mrs Green drag Emily into the house. As the Chauffeur takes the car away, Oscar enters on a bicycle. He dismounts, out of breath. He stares at the house, then goes off round the side, pushing his bike. The scene changes and we are now indoors where there is a smart evening-dress ball in progress. Several dancers are on the floor. Clara, now aged sixty-six and looking very like her mother Charity, is dancing with Nigel Chatterton-Brown, a very English-looking, slightly red-faced, country gent. A live (offstage) dance band is playing, of whom we only see the leader/vocalist.

Emily staggers in, as though pushed into the room. She watches open-mouthed.

SONG: 'OUT OF SIGHT' (LIVE REPRISE)

Vocalist
Can't get you out of my sight,
Can't shake you, try as I might.
I see you morning and night,
How you pursue me.

Though sadly, sorry to say
Despite my finest display,
My darling, try as I may,
You look straight through me.

For you
I am merely some illusion
Fleeting as the morning mist.
It's true,
I am under no delusion,
Clearly I do not exist.

Been this way since it began.
Sweet lady, please if you can,
Take pity on this invisible man.

TWO-VERSE INSTRUMENTAL: DANCE BREAK

Take note
Of this sorry apparition –

Surely love can't be this blind?
To quote
In the words of my optician
Out of sight means out of mind.

It's not so hard if you try,
You just need open an eye,
Have mercy on this invisible guy.

The dance finishes. Polite applause. The band goes into another slower number. Clara sees Emily and crosses to her.

Clara (*gushingly charming*) Emily! At last! How lovely! They told me they'd found you. We were beginning to wonder if you'd ever arrive. Mind you, I was sure you would eventually. (*kissing her*) Welcome, dear. Are you hungry at all? Would you like something to eat? There's masses of food. Of course, a lot of things are desperately hard to get hold of these days, thanks to this bloody war, but fortunately we do have one or two very good friends in the Ministry of Food, so we're terribly lucky. How are you? Tell me all your news? It's been simply years! Well, it has for all of us, it's probably only been a matter of minutes as far as you're concerned, hasn't it?

Emily (*staring at her, uncertain*) Aunt Charity?

Clara Oh no, darling. No. Aunt Charity – Mother died twenty years ago, alas. But then she was never terribly strong, was she, poor thing?

Emily Then you are – you are –

Clara Clara! Didn't you recognise me? Have I changed so much? I suppose I must have done. You haven't changed at all, of course, Cousin Emily. Still the same gawky little creature, aren't you? Come. There's someone who's dying to meet you. This way.

Clara propels Emily into another room. The music recedes but continues under.

We have got some simply gorgeous vintage champagne, by the way. God knows where it came from – oh no, what am I saying? You can't possibly be drinking yet, can you? Silly me. Now, wait there, one second. Don't run away, will you? Besides, where could you go?

Clara laughs and goes. Emily stands awkwardly in the middle of the large room. There is a gaming table with a roulette wheel.

Emily (*to herself*) I will wake up in a minute, I know I will. This is all a nightmare. It must be.

Lucas, now nearly ninety, enters on two walking sticks. He stops in the doorway as he sees Emily. Clara hovers behind him.

Lucas Emily, my dear . . .

Emily stares.

Don't you remember me? What do you make of that, Clara? I don't think she even remembers me.

Clara It's your Uncle Lucas, Emily. You haven't forgotten my father, surely?

Emily draws back slightly.

Lucas No, Emily hasn't forgotten, Clara. As far as she's concerned, it can't have been that long ago since we last met, can it? Don't be alarmed, my dear, for me that was way in the distant past. All forgotten, eh?

Emily Do you expect me to forget that you killed Uncle Martin?

Lucas Did I? Did I now? You know, when you get to my age, Emily – you must appreciate I'm nearly ninety now – one does tend to forget. One is, after all, too busy desperately clinging to the present to bother with the past that much. Let's not quarrel, Emily. All I require from you is the Machine which brought you here. With that, you see, I also control my future . . .

Emily You shall never have the Machine. It was Uncle Martin's . . .

Lucas Indeed it was. Unfortunately, though, owing to Martin's tragic murder – his assistant Bob was subsequently tried and hanged for it, by the way –

Emily Bob was?

Lucas – due to that and to your own totally inexplicable disappearance back in 1886, everything Martin owned passed to me. Thus, in fact, the Machine is mine. I am having it collected as we speak. So. Enjoy the party, young lady, why not? Let bygones be bygones, eh? Have you been admiring my house? Isn't it magnificent? Since you left, I'm delighted to say, Emily, that fortune has smiled upon me.

He stands close to Emily having steadily advanced and trapped her in a corner. Clara watches, amused.

Emily I do not know how you have managed to become as rich as this. But I am certain it was not through any honest means.

Lucas (*amused*) Emily! How could you? Shall I tell you my little secret?

SONG: 'DEAL'

(*softly*) I have a certain method, I confess,
Upon which I have based my mad success –
No matter if it's cards or booze or drugs –
The Stock Exchange, or wholesale doodlebugs . . .
My secret, which I happily reveal,
Is make sure in this game of life, you deal.

I need to deal–
To wrap my fingers round that pack.
I need to feel
Whilst I'm distributing the stack,
As other players hope to win,
I'll fix the odds and rake it in –
I love to deal.

Observe me deal.
It's very simple, please believe,
Pas difficile!
With several aces up your sleeve.
So let the game of chance begin.
I know which numbers every spin
Will soon reveal –
I've fixed the wheel!

I love to deal.
It's only fools who trust to fate.
Just hear them squeal
As I take candy off their plate.
It's elementary indeed
As they display a naked greed
They can't conceal –

Clara
He loves to deal.

Lucas
You'll never win, it's far too hard . . .

Clara
The odds aren't real . . .

Lucas
I've marked the back of every card –

Clara
He's not a man you ever beat –

Emily
    'Cos he's a liar and a cheat
    Who loves to steal –
    Not one ideal . . .

Lucas
    For when I deal . . .

All
    . . . I deal.

Emily (*defiantly*) Anyone who profits from the death of others must be a very sorry person indeed. And I think your house is thoroughly vulgar and in poor taste. I would not wish to live here a minute longer than I have to.

Lucas (*smiling unpleasantly*) Nor will you, my dear. Nor will you.

At this point, Nigel enters. He stops as he sees Emily. Nigel's English pronunciation is flawless but his syntax is occasionally a bit dodgy.

Nigel Oh, I'm sorry, I do beg your pardon –

Lucas Ah, Mr Chatterton-Brown! Dear chap, do come in and meet my niece, Emily.

Nigel Good lord, what a delightful little cherub, how do you do?

Lucas Mr Chatterton-Brown is a business partner, Emily. I trust you'll be civil to him.

Nigel I'm sure she will. She looks a well-raised little girl to me. And what an attractive turn-up she's wearing, isn't it charming? Well-shaped hair. Nice rosy cheeks. I can see you've been consuming your carrots like a good child, haven't you?

Emily (*a bit baffled*) I beg your pardon?

Nigel What's wrong? You look a little down in the teeth, eh?

Nigel pinches Emily's cheek. Emily responds by biting his hand. Nigel snatches his hand away.

(*angrily*) Das kleine Biest! Sie hat mich in die Hand gebissen!

Clara (*simultaneously*) Emily!

A slight pause as they're aware that Nigel has rather blown his cover.

Lucas (*suavely*) In English, if you please, Mr Brown.

Nigel (*laughing*) By jove! The filly packs a bit of a nip, eh? (*wagging his finger jovially at Emily*) Naughty girl!

Clara Would you care for some more champagne, Nigel?

Nigel That would be absolutely first-hole, thank you, Clara. First-hole!

Lucas (*murmuring*) Rate.

Clara refills their glasses during the next.

Nigel We must lift our glasses and grill our new deal, Lucas.

Lucas Toast. Yes, indeed we must. It has been a pleasure doing business with you, Mr Brown.

Nigel Well, in times of crisis we English should all glue together, shouldn't we?

Lucas Stick. Yes, we certainly should. Your health!

Clara Cheers!

Nigel *Auf euer Wohl!*

Lucas In English, if you please, Mr Brown.

Emily I may be young – I may not know much about what is going on – but I know enough to see that you're all foul, disgusting – traitors. And I am going to find a policeman!

Emily makes a dart for the door.

Clara Oh, no!

Clara catches Emily easily and grips her arm. Emily struggles.

You bite me, young woman, and I promise you it will be the last thing you ever bite in your life.

Emily It probably will be! If I bit you I would probably be poisoned!

Clara (*angrily*) Why, you little –!

Lucas That's enough, Clara, that's enough!

Nigel What do you plot to do with her? She knows numerous things, surely.

Lucas Don't concern yourself, Mr Brown. Fortunately, this little girl vanished over fifty years ago – so no one's going to miss her now, are they?

Nigel I don't understand. What are you explaining?

Lucas It doesn't matter.

Nigel I don't know, I spend five years learning to speak fluid English in our finest German university and I still find people are pulling the wool over my ears.

Clara What shall I do with her, Father?

Lucas Put her in the cellar. Mr Green will deal with her. That's what we pay him for, after all. Goodbye, Emily. And this time it really is goodbye.

Nigel (*in an undertone*) One minute!

Clara What is it?

Nigel Act conventionally. I think there is someone lingering outside the window frames.

Nigel moves to the french window and suddenly and swiftly pulls it open. Oscar almost falls into the room.

Lucas Who the devil are you?

Oscar (*recovering swiftly*) Alright! Nobody move!

Clara instinctively releases Emily, who moves away to another corner.

Lucas What were you doing out there?

Oscar (*pointing to his armband*) I am an official ARP warden, conducting a blackout check. Who are you?

Lucas I am Sir Lucas Lashmore, the owner of this house.

Oscar Oh, are you indeed? In that case, I am holding you responsible.

Lucas Responsible?

Oscar Are you aware there is a war on? Have you never heard of blackout regulations? This place is like the Eddystone Lighthouse. It's lit up like a Christmas tree out there! Attract every enemy plane for miles.

Lucas Nonsense!

Oscar You don't believe me, go outside and have a look for yourself.

Lucas Certainly not! Can't you see I have guests? There is no problem with our blackout. We are always most careful . . .

Oscar Alright, you switch the lights off in here for a second. You'll find moonlight streaming through those windows. (*to Clara*) You! Switch the lights off!

Clara (*startled*) Very well.

Lucas (*realising something is wrong*) Clara! Wait! No, don't switch off the –

The room is plunged into darkness.

Oscar Emily! Quickly! Take my hand!

Nigel (*simultaneously*) *Was ist? Was ist hier los?*

Clara (*simultaneously*) Where are you taking that girl?

Lucas (*simultaneously*) In English, Mr Brown! Stop them! Don't let them leave the house . . .

The lights cross-fade to the street. It is dimly lit by moonlight. Oscar enters, dragging Emily.

Emily What are you doing here? Where are we going?

Oscar Anywhere away from there, love. Cheer up! I followed you on me bike.

Emily Your what?

Oscar My bicycle.

Emily You have a bicycle! I've always wanted to ride a bicycle!

Oscar Now's your chance! Come on, I'll give you a ride!

A loud wailing from the warning air-raid siren.

Oh, no. Forget it

Emily (*covering her ears*) What is that noise?

Oscar Change of plan. Air-raid warning. We'd better get to the shelter. Unless you want to get blown up along with everything else. I thought you might have had enough for one evening.

Emily Please, wait! I still don't understand. What is an air raid? What are we sheltering from?

The drone of bombers approaching overhead.

Oscar (*pointing*) Those things up there, my love, that's what. (*pointing*) See?

Emily (*craning her neck, alarmed*) What are they? What on earth are *they*?

Oscar Enemy aeroplanes. German bombers! Run for it!

Emily needs no second bidding. They dash through the streets. The sounds of ack-ack batteries again. Distant bombs exploding.
Emily and Oscar reach the shelter.

Emily (*as they enter*) Is this where we were before?

Oscar Right.

Emily (*reading*) Goodge Street. What is a goodge . . . ? Ah!

A loud bang much closer this time. Oscar drags her inside. They finally stop, breathless.

Oscar (*regaining his breath*) That's better!

Emily Thank you, Mr –?

Oscar Oscar. Oscar Fieldman.

Emily Emily Bonny. (*She extends her hand.*) Thank you for rescuing me.

Oscar We'll be safe enough down here. Soon as the all-clear sounds, we'll go to the police station. Put in a report.

Emily About Uncle Lucas?

Oscar You were right about one thing. He's certainly a traitor, love. I'm sorry if he's your uncle but . . . Well, he's worse, he's a war profiteer. Doesn't bother him which side he's on. That's the lowest of the low, believe me. He's one of the reasons we're up against it the way we are.

Emily Are we?

Oscar Between us, things aren't too good. Nobody likes to say it out loud, but the way things are going, the whole thing could be over in a week.

Emily Over?

Oscar This could be an occupied country, love. First time since the Norman invasion. Think of that.

Emily Oh. How terrible! I thought we ruled the waves.

Oscar Not any more, we don't. Never mind! Cheer up! Listen, Emily, what's going on? Where do you come from? Why are those people after you?

Emily It is – complicated.

Oscar Yes, I gathered.

Emily I am not certain you would believe me if I told you.

Oscar Try me. Go on.

Emily The year now is –?

Oscar The year now? Gawd help us! 1940, love.

Emily Then I have travelled – let me see – fifty-four years forward in time.

Oscar In time?

Emily Yes.

Oscar You're looking very good on it.

Emily You see? You will never believe me! I was born in March 1877, I am now nine years old and I have travelled forward in time from the year 1886. (*Slight pause.*) You do not believe me, do you?

Oscar I was hanging on for the other explanation, that's all, love. I'm finding this one a bit hard to –

Emily I will show you the Machine. Maybe that will convince you.

Oscar That'll be your – your Time Machine, I take it?

Emily It was invented by my Uncle Martin. Uncle Lucas must not be allowed to have it. Things seem bad enough. I dread to think what would happen.

Oscar Come on then. You show me, eh?

Emily I hope it is still here. I know they were planning to move it.

Oscar (*gamely humouring her*) No, we can't have that, can we?

They reach the emergency door. They enter cautiously.

(*looking around, much relieved*) Oh, dear! It seems to have gone. What a surprise! You had me going there for a minute, Emily Bonny! I almost believed you. Pity. I'd like to have seen it, really.

Emily You can.

Oscar What?

Emily It is still here.

Oscar Where?

Emily (*indicating*) Here. See? In the floor.

Oscar In the floor?

Emily You just have to stand here, you see. Look, I will show you.

Emily is about to lead Oscar onto the Portal when Mr and Mrs Green step from the shadows.

Mrs Green Thank you, dear. That's saved us a lot of bother. We were just trying to figure that out, actually.

Mr Green How did you get back here, anyway?

Mrs Green What's it matter? We'll just have to take her home again, won't we?

Emily (*to Oscar*) Quickly! Step on here!

Oscar Where?

Emily (*stepping onto the Portal*) Here!

Mr Green (*producing a gun*) Stand still! Don't move!

Oscar Emily, we'd better do as we're told. That's a gun. I don't know if you've seen a gun before but –

Emily Yes, Oscar, I do know what a gun is – Come along!

Oscar (*stepping onto the Portal*) No, well, all I'm saying is –

The Portal wall starts to rise.

Oh, stripe me!

Mr Green (*raising the gun*) I'm warning you!

Mrs Green Don't shoot, for God's sake, Alf! You'll damage the Machine!

Mr and Mrs Green move forward. The sounds start, as before, and the lights flash. Emily fiddles with the control panel.

Emily (*from within the Machine*) Hold tight . . .!

Oscar (*a long-drawn-out wail*) Help!

The Machine travels forward again. Darkness. Mr and Mrs Green disappear.
  In a moment, it stops and the wall lowers.
  Oscar is crouching, his hands round his head.

Emily (*looking about her*) Where are we now? I think we have moved forward again. I cannot make this machine go backwards. Uncle Martin was right. (*aware of Oscar*) Oscar? Are you hurt! Oscar!

Oscar (*emerging*) Where are we?

Emily I am uncertain. Somewhere in the future, I presume . . .

Oscar I don't believe it. You mean we've – we've actually travelled – through *time*? It was all *true*?

Emily Of course. I told you, Oscar.

Oscar (*laughing a little hysterically*) Sorry, I'm – I'm having a bit of a problem with this. I am standing here in the future, right? In my own future?

Emily Both our futures.

Oscar So – er . . . Let me get this straight. Cheer up! If I'm in my own future what happens if I meet myself?

Emily (*pondering this*) I do not think you could possibly meet yourself, Oscar, because – let me see – that would assume you were still there but you aren't because you have travelled here. And if you are no longer there, you could not possibly meet yourself here.

Oscar No?

Emily No. The problem would only arise if you travel back beyond the point when you disappeared. Because I suppose that then you *could* meet yourself because you would still be there. You would not yet have travelled forward. You would have travelled backwards to a time before you travelled forwards, you see?

Oscar Ah yes, but – if I hadn't yet – how come I was –? Unless I –? No, wait if I –? (*Slight pause.*) No, I'm lost.

Emily (*tiring a little of all this*) Oscar, since this machine appears unable to travel backwards, the problem will hardly arise. Shall we go?

Oscar (*alarmed*) Where?

Emily We must find someone. To ask where – when we are.

Oscar Emily. I have to say this. I am considerably frightened.

Emily So am I. I am terrified. What of it? Who would not be?

Oscar No, you don't understand – in my case – it's – it's – how shall I put this? – I'm a natural coward, you see –

Emily Oscar, just now, you were extremely brave! You saved my life!

Oscar Well, that was – I saw them threatening you – and – I couldn't help myself.

Emily That is known as courage, Oscar.

Oscar No, Emily – that is known as lunacy, that's quite different. In that war back there, the one they're all fighting . . . I should be part of that. I'm able-bodied, I'm fit. Why aren't I out there with the rest of our brave lads? Because of my feet, that's why.

Emily Your feet?

Oscar I've got funny feet. I needn't have told them about them but I did and when they knew I had funny feet they took one look at them and they wouldn't take me.

Emily They don't look very funny to me.

Oscar Just pray you don't ever meet me with my socks off, that's all. Anyway, now we're losing the war – lost the war practically – and I should have been there. But I wasn't because I was too scared to go and fight.

Music under.

Emily (*solemnly*) Oscar, you are one of the bravest people I have ever met. Believe me, there are moments when all of us could have been braver. Back there, I ran away because I was frightened. I could have prevented my uncle's death but instead I chose to run away.

Oscar Cheer up! You seem brave enough to me, Emily.

Emily (*shrugging modestly*) Well ..

SONG: 'WHENEVER' (REPRISE)

Whenever I'm afraid,
When I'm alone,
With not a soul to guide me,
To see me through the night
And whisper everything's all right.
Although there's no special place can hide me
From all the fear of the dark inside me –
It won't seem long till everything
Becomes as bright as day.

Both
I know the sun will rise,
That come the dawn
I tell myself, as sure as day breaks,
I will laugh away my fears –
Whenever I'm afraid.

Emily (*extending her hand*) Are you coming with me, now?

Oscar (*with new courage*) Try and stop me! (*He takes her hand.*)

From the shadows the sound of something approaching.

They freeze. Droid 3 appears. It stops and begins to emit a beeping sound.

(*terrified to death*) Oh, stripe me pink!

Emily Whenever are we *now*?

The lights fade on the encounter as the beeping leads into music.

End of Act One.

Act Two

Entr'acte leads into the alarm from Droid 3 as before. Oscar and Emily are staring at it.

Oscar (*in a whisper*) What are we going to do?

Emily It has not tried to attack us. I suppose that is one consolation.

Oscar Probably because it's about to blow up.

Emily Do you think so?

Oscar In my experience things that go beep-beep-beep usually blow up.

Emily Perhaps we should attempt to communicate with it. (*rather awkwardly*) Good day. My name is Emily Jane Elizabeth Seymore Catherine Charity Prudence Caroline Bonny.

The Droid continues its alarm.

Oscar I don't think it can hear you, Emily.

Emily (*impatient, loudly*) Perhaps if it stopped making that noise it might do!

Oscar Are those really all your names?

Emily Yes, of course. I don't use all of them, though.

Oscar No, I can see you wouldn't. Lot of names, isn't it?

Emily Is it? How many names do you have?

Oscar Two. Oscar John.

Emily Is that all?

Oscar I'm from a deprived family. My parents couldn't afford any imagination.

Droids 1 and 2 appear from different directions. They look very like Droid 3.

Emily (*seeing them first*) Oscar . . . there's more of them!

Droid 3 stops its racket. Silence.

Oscar (*softly*) I can see. Now what?

There is a series of quick-fire bursts of digital chatter between the three Droids.

Emily What are they doing?

Oscar They seem to be having a chat. Hang on! (*He moves forward slightly.*) Hello . . . Excuse me!

The machines wheel round and stare at him.

(*nervously*) Cheer up! Fancy a sing-song, do you? All together now! (*singing*) Don't you ever let a ratter eat his dinner off your platter . . . Aaaaah!

Rapidly, the three Droids close in and surround Oscar. Instruments and probes extend from them. They examine him, chattering as they do so.

Emily (*during this*) Oscar, are you alright?

Oscar makes a series of wailing sounds.

Are they hurting you?

Oscar Noo – oo – oo – oo – oo . . .

Emily What's the matter then?

Oscar They're . . . ooo . . . oooh . . . ooo . . . tickling me! Oooo!

The Droids finish with Oscar and have a further quick chatter together.

Emily I do not know why you have to make quite so much noise, Oscar! I do not believe that anyone can possibly be that – ahh! Oooh!

The three Droids have swiftly surrounded Emily and started their same procedure again.

Ooooo – oooo – oooo – ooo – ooo! Stop it! Stop it, at once! Ooooo!

Oscar (*triumphantly*) Ah-ha! You see?

The Droids finish with Emily. They move away and huddle in beeping consultation.

Emily (*her dignity affronted*) Heavens above! Really!

Oscar I think they were giving us a medical. You know, like the army.

Emily I have never been in the army, Oscar.

Oscar Neither have I. 'Cos of my funny feet.

Emily (*impatiently*) So you told me.

Sudden silence as the Droids stop chattering. Droid 1 steps forward.

Droid 1 You – are – human.

Emily Of course we are human.

Droid 1 Please confirm.

Emily We could have told you that, instead of poking and prodding us.

Droid 1 Please confirm.

Oscar We confirm.

Another burst of exuberant chatter.

There they go again!

Quite unexpectedly, the three Droids burst into brief song.

SONG: 'THE HUMAN WELCOME SONG'

Droids
Every Droid
Is overjoyed
To welcome you
Dear humanoid.

Emily and Oscar stand rather awkwardly whilst they are serenaded.

Emily (*during this*) I feel rather like one of our African explorers.

As the song ends, Emily feels that perhaps a speech of acknowledgement is in order.

(*formally*) We thank you, from the bottom of our hearts, all of you, for your warm and gracious welcome. We bring greetings from Her Majesty Queen Victoria and –

Oscar – and much love from George the Sixth as well, thank you.

Droid 1 We are here to serve you . . .

Droids 2 and 3 Serve you . . .

Emily Thank you. And who are you?

Droid 1 We are Preservers.

Emily Preservers? You mean you make jam?

Oscar No, I don't think so, Emily. What exactly do you preserve?

Droid 2 Life.

Droid 3 Human life.

Oscar Good. And – er – why do we need preserving, especially? I mean, is there still a war on, is there?

Droid 1 Oh, no . . .

Droid 2 . . . no . . .

Droid 3 . . . no war.

Droid 1 War . . .

Droid 2 . . . is . . .

Droid 3 . . . forbidden.

Emily Good. I am glad to hear it. About time too!

Oscar Then why do you need to preserve us?

Droids (*together*) You are an endangered species.

Emily An endangered species?

Droid 1 Rare!

Droids 2 and 3 (*together*) Very, very rare.

Oscar But, let's get this straight, there are other humans living here?

Droids (*together*) Oh yes!

Emily So how many are here?

Droid 1 One!

Emily One?

Droid 2 Char Tee was all we were able to save.

Droid 3 From the final war.

Droids (*together*) Little Char Tee . . .

Emily Who is Char Tee?

Droid 1 She's . . .

Droid 2 ... *our* ...

Droid 3 ... human.

Emily May we meet her?

Droids (*together*) Of course!

Droid 1 You must ...

Droid 2 ... interface ...

Droid 3 ... with her.

Emily We must what?

Droid 1 After decontamination.

Oscar Beg pardon?

Droid 2 Step this way ...

Droid 3 Thank you ...

Oscar is bustled to another corner of the room. The next section quite rapidly:

Droid 1 Keep very still!

Droid 2 Very, very still!

Droid 3 Thank you!

Droid 1 Commence decontamination!

Droid 2 Commencing!

Droid 3 Go!

Oscar I don't know what all this is about I'm suuuuurrrre ... !

Oscar drops through the floor and vanishes.

Emily Oscar? Oscar? What have you done with my friend?

Droid 1 He'll be back . . .

Droid 2 . . . very soon . . .

Droid 3 . . . don't worry!

Emily Where has he gone?

Droid 1 You're next!

Droid 2 Join the queue!

Droids (*together*) Thank you!

Emily Oh no, I am definitely not next.

Droid 1 It . . .

Droid 2 . . . is . . .

Droid 3 . . . necessary.

Droids (*together*) You may be contaminated.

Emily I am certainly not contaminated! I would welcome a good hot bath if there is one available but that is all I require, thank you very much.

Droid 1 You are human . . .

Droid 2 . . . and you have been outside . . .

Droid 3 It is . . .

Droid 1 . . . possible . . .

Droid 2 . . . you are . . .

Droid 3 . . . contaminated.

Droid 1 The air outside . . .

Droid 2 . . . is poisonous

Droid 3 . . . for humans.

Droids (*together*) It is necessary.

Emily I haven't even been outside, I don't see how we can have been . . .

Oscar pops back through the floor. He is slightly red in the face. He is now dressed in a silver boiler suit.

Oscar Stripe me pink!

Droids (*together*) Decontamination complete!

Droid 1 Thank you!

Droid 2 Next please!

Droid 3 This way!

Droids (*together*) Thank you!

Emily hesitates.

Oscar It's – not too bad, Emily. You get a good scrubbing! Go on! At least then they'll let us meet – whoever it is. She might be able to help us.

Emily (*stepping forward, reluctantly*) Oh. Very well.

Droid 1 Thank you!

Droid 2 Next please!

Droid 3 This way!

Droids (*together*) Thank you!

Emily I must warn you that certain types of soap make me sneeeeeezzzze . . .!

Emily drops through the floor.

Oscar Be careful with her, she's special.

Droids (*together*) All humans are special.

At this point Ziggi (Android Z1991) arrives. It is similar to the others but slightly more battered. It beeps excitedly.

Droid 1 Model Z1991, please observe we are in speech mode. We have humans present.

Ziggi Humans? (*excitedly, seeing Oscar*) Hello, hello, hello! Humans! I say, I say, I say ...

> Every Droid
> Is overjoyed
> To –

Droid 1 Model Z1991, where have you been?

Droid 2 Did you not hear the alarm?

Droid 3 From Alpha 665?

Ziggi I was reading.

Droids (*together*) Reading?

Ziggi The books.

Droid 1 Z1991, why were you scanning ...

Droid 2 ... human ...

Droid 3 ... books?

Ziggi I wanted to learn. Tiddly-pom.

Droid 1 Illogical!

Droids 1 and 2 (*together*) Illogical!

Droids (*together*) Illogical!

Droid 1 There is nothing more to learn, Z1991.

Droid 2 Our knowledge is complete.

Droid 3 We are complete. There is nothing we can learn from books.

Droids (*together*) Books are for humans.

Ziggi I have been reading *Winnie the Pooh* –

Droid 1 Winnie . . .

Droid 2 . . . the . . .

Droid 3 . . . Pooh?

Droid 1 Unstable deviation!

Droid 2 Invalid system entry!

Droid 3 Re-boot!

Ziggi I am perfectly stable.

Oscar It's a good book, *Winnie the Pooh*.

Ziggi Yes! Oh, you bear of little brain!

Oscar My dad used to read it to me.

Ziggi I have no dad.

Oscar No. I'm sorry.

Ziggi Would you read it to me?

Droid 1 (*sharply*) Z1991! Deviation! That is enough!

Droids (*together*) Decontamination complete!

Emily pops up again. Hers is a total transformation. She wears a similar outfit to Oscar. Gone are her curls and ringlets. Her hair is now cropped short.

Oscar (*incredulously*) Emily? Is that you, Emily?

Emily (*outraged*) What have you done to me? What have you done?

Droid 1 We will now . . .

Droid 2 . . . bring . . .

Droid 3 . . . Char Tee!

Droids 2 and 3 go off.

Emily (*in despair*) What have they done to my hair?

Oscar It's not so bad, Emily. It quite suits you. Cheer up. It looks good.

Emily (*only slightly mollified*) Where I come from, the only women with hair like this are lunatics or ones with severe head lice.

Oscar Well, give it time . . .

Ziggi You never know, it'll probably grow on you . . . (*It laughs.*)

Emily (*huffily*) I am sorry. I do not find that at all funny.

Droid 1 Z1991, reconfigure!

Ziggi Reconfigured!

'How sweet to be a Cloud
Floating in the Blue-Blue-Blue-Blue-Blue-Blue!'

Droid 1 Reconfigure!

Ziggi Reconfigured!

Droid 1 leaves for a moment.

Emily What is it talking about?

Oscar It's a book. It was quoting from a book. It's called *Winnie the Pooh*.

Ziggi *Winnie the Pooh!*

Emily (*doubtfully*) Really? Is it elevating?

Oscar It's funny.

Emily Then I do not think I would care for it. I only read books that are elevating.

Oscar Emily, how old did you say you were?

Emily I am nine, I told you.

Oscar Well, there are times when you seem more like ninety.

Emily I do not understand that remark, Oscar.

Oscar Fun! Have some fun, girl. You're a kid! Have fun!

Emily I am not a kid. Life is a serious business, Oscar. Anyway, I certainly could not begin to have fun dressed like this.

Oscar Why not?

Emily Because it – it is improper. My . . . are showing.

Oscar Your what?

Emily (*whispering*) My – upper legs –

Oscar Your upper legs! You mean your –

Emily Shhh!

Oscar I won't look. Promise.

Emily You are laughing at me.

Oscar I'm sorry. You come from a different time with different values and I shouldn't laugh. I'm sorry. Cheer up, there's probably people in – I don't know – 1995 – who'd laugh at me.

Emily (*icily*) I hope that by then they will have learnt better manners.

Oscar (*extending his hand*) Sorry. Forgive me?

Emily (*shaking his hand*) I forgive you.

Oscar Hey, look out –

Droids 2 and 3 return. They bring on Char Tee (Charity) in a type of hi-tec sedan chair. She is seated at a computer-style keyboard. She is protected by an enclosed clear screen. Droid 1 simultaneously returns with a free-standing keyboard on a portable plinth.

Droids
   Every Droid
   Is overjoyed
   To welcome you
   Dear humanoid.

Oscar (*during this*) Here we go again!

Droid 1 You may interface with Char Tee.

Emily (*examining the keyboard*) What is this thing?

Droid 1 A communicator. You are unfamiliar?

Emily I have no idea what it is at all.

Oscar Ah, let me. Yes, it's a sort of – er – it's a sort of typewriter. You type on it . . . like that. (*He mimes.*)

Emily You do? To what end? Why are all the letters in the wrong order?

Oscar Ah! There's a very sound reason for that.

Emily Is there?

Oscar But I've no idea what it is.

Emily Ridiculous! Can't we simply talk to her?

Droid 2 You must interface through the keyboard.

Droid 3 That is how Char Tee communicates.

Emily How stupid . . .

Droid 1 All humans interface. We will leave you to communicate.

The three Droids and Ziggi leave. A pause.

Oscar We'd better say something to her, I suppose. What shall we say?

Emily (*faintly sarcastic*) Hello?

Oscar Good idea. (*He attempts to type.*) Ooops! Hang on. Excuse me, I'm not used to this. Back in my time this is a woman's job.

Emily Presumably they're the only ones intelligent enough to use it.

Oscar I'll ignore that. (*typing laboriously*) H – look for an A . . .

Emily What do you want an A for?

Oscar I'm writing hallo.

Emily It is spelt H – *E* . . . H – E – L – L – O.

Oscar No, H – *A* . . .

Emily H – *E* . . . (*typing for him*) E! There! Now L? Find an L. Ridiculous!

They both hunt for the L.

Both (*finding it together*) L! (*Slight pause.*) L! (*They type the second L.*)

Oscar O? Where's the O?

They hunt.

(*a fraction ahead of Emily*) O!

Emily O!

They study their result.

Now we've got two O's.

Oscar Helloo! Why isn't she saying anything?

Emily (*considering*) Hmmm!

Emily studies the keyboard and then presses a key. Immediately, Char Tee starts a flurry of rapid typing. Music under.

SONG: 'COMMUNICATION'

Oscar What did you do?

Emily I pressed that one there. This one. 'Enter.'

Oscar How d'you know to do that?

Emily Merely a guess.

Oscar (*studying their screen*) Hey, look, look!

Both (*reading*)
Hailgreet! Hailgreet!!
I please you meet!
Describe you, answer to my prayer,
What age?
Which sex?
Who know?
Who care?

Emily (*speaking*) This is the most ridiculous way to communicate I have ever known in my life!

Oscar (*speaking*) Hang on! Hang on!

(*typing*) Hailgreet! Hailgreet!
We please you meet!
We're over here, look up, look-see.

Emily
I'm girl.

Oscar
I'm man.

Emily
Look him.

Oscar
Look me.

Emily (*speaking*) Look! Look, look, look, look, look, look!

Char Tee
How big? How small?

Emily
I'm short.

Oscar
I'm tall.

Char Tee
How fat? How thin?

Emily
We're normal size.

Char Tee
You dark?

Emily
No, fair.

Char Tee
What colour eyes?

Emily (*speaking, frustratedly*) Red with yellow stripes! Oh, this is going to take for ever!

Oscar and Emily go back to their keyboard. Char Tee sings to herself.

Char Tee
Here's to friend
Unknown, unseen,
To bigworld friend
On small dark screen.
People hurt you,
Lie, desert you,
People use you,
Harm confuse you,

People ask too much.
People reach out touch.
Here's to love,
Allpure allclean,
My bigtrue love
On small dark screen.

Oscar (*trying again*)
Hailgreet! Hailgreet!
I do repeat –

Emily
I don't know why we're typing this.
Me here –

Oscar
You there –

Emily
Close man –

Oscar
Near miss –

Char Tee
Hailgreet! Hailgreet!
I you entreat
No talk face-face now not since war,
No see
No hear
No touch –

Emily (*who's had enough*) No more!

Emily strides towards Char Tee and opens her glass container.

Listen, enough of this! I am Emily, how do you do?

Char Tee (*retreating from Emily, outraged*) How dare! Come you do that! Are you un-mannered? Communicate, properspeak me!

Emily I wish to talk to you. We have things to ask you. I am sure you have things you would like to ask us. Let us sit and talk, please.

Char Tee What say? Properspeak, that way. Not this way.

Emily No, this way is quicker. That way is too long.

Char Tee No. That way quick. Quicksafe. (*miming a word, jumping from keyboard to keyboard*) Word – word. Word – word. See?

Emily No! (*miming between her own mouth and Char Tee's ear*) Word – word! Word – word!

Char Tee (*retreating more*) No, no. Not good. Speakvirus.

Oscar Virus?

Char Tee Infect. Not we talk word – word – (*demonstrating Emily's method*) – no!

Emily Yes.

Char Tee Elsefight!

Emily Fight?

Char Tee No good meet. Allfight.

Emily We don't want to fight.

Char Tee Human all fight. Must fight. My mum/dad diefight. Char Tee mum/dad, see?

Emily Yes? Your mother and father died in a fight?

Char Tee Char Tee grandmum/dad diefight. Great grandmum/dad diefight. Great great grandmum/dad. Allfight. Allfight since lordknowsLucas.

Emily Since who?

Char Tee LordknowsLucas.

Emily Lucas? You are related to Lucas? Lucas – you?

Char Tee Lucas. Threegreats. Lucas.

Emily (*to Oscar*) I believe she is saying that Uncle Lucas is her great-great-great-grandfather . . . (*to Char Tee*) Three greats, yes?

Char Tee Yes. Check. Great-great-great-grandmum/dad. Lucas and Char Tee.

Emily Charity. You mean Charity. Aunt Charity?

Char Tee Char Tee, yes. I too Char Tee.

Emily Then we are related. I am your first, second, third – heavens, maybe fourth – cousin, I can't work it out. Cousin! Me! (*She extends a hand.*)

Char Tee No! No allfight!

Emily No, not fight. Friend!

Oscar We're friends. It's alright!

Char Tee (*hysterically*) No hurt Char Tee! No hurt Char Tee!

Emily I am not going to hurt you! For goodness sake!

Emily grabs Char Tee's arm. Char Tee goes completely wild, struggling and flailing to get free. She backs into a corner, screaming.
  The three Droids and Ziggi all appear from various directions, beeping furiously.

Oscar What's the matter with her?

Droids 2 and 3 are calming Char Tee. They spray her arm with a sedative. She calms down.

Emily (*to Droid 1*) We did nothing to her, I promise. We were only talking.

Droid 1 You directspoke to her. She is not prepared. You must use properspeak. Humans are forbidden directspeak.

Emily You mean she never speaks to anyone directly? She's always on her own?

Char Tee is led away by Droids 2 and 3.

Droid 1 The programme is correctly adjusted. Humans must be separated to prevent war. You too must be separated. You are unstable. I will obtain authority. Z1991, remain to watch them.

Droid 1 goes. Ziggi remains.

Oscar Separated? Oy! Wait! You can't separate us . . . Do you hear that? They're going to separate us. They're . . . (*seeing Emily*) Emily?

Emily is very thoughtful.

You alright?

Emily How lonely! How terrifyingly lonely for her.

Oscar Maybe she – maybe she's used to – being on her own. Perhaps.

Emily No, you never get used to loneliness, Oscar. Never. Believe me.

Oscar No. I don't suppose you do.

Emily Oscar, we have to go back. I have to go back. If this, this *now*, is what happens, then I have to return to my own time. Uncle Lucas must be stopped. That girl, Char Tee – Charity – she is my distant relative, Oscar. I cannot bear to think of her living the rest of her life in this manner. So lonely. So alone. What way is that to live?

Oscar But what can you do?

Emily It must be possible to undo things. It must. To alter them somehow? It must be, Oscar. The world cannot end like this. It is up to us to change things. Because each of us, in our way, has caused it to become like this. Yes, you may say people like Uncle Lucas were mainly responsible – but it was truly all of us. Uncle Lucas only did the things he did because we allowed him. We never tried to stop him. Because we were afraid of him. Or maybe it was just easier to ignore him or simply to run away. But, the further we run, Oscar, the further into the future we try to hide, the more we shall witness the effects of what people like Uncle Lucas have done. I know it.

Oscar (*considering this*) You're right. 'Course you are. One problem, though. That thing can't go backwards, can it?

Emily It must do. It must.

Oscar Unless time only goes one way, like. And that machine – just makes it go a bit quicker.

Emily (*appalled*) Then we can never go back.

Oscar It's just a theory. (*to Ziggi*) Excuse me. Do you happen to know anything about time?

Ziggi It's about time you asked me that.

Ziggi laughs. They don't. It stops.

Only joking. Reconfigure! What do you wish to know?

Emily We wish to know if time only travel forwards. Or does it ever travel backwards?

Ziggi (*after beeping for a bit*) There is considerable data regarding time. Do you wish me to decompress and start unloading?

Oscar How long will that take?

Ziggi Approximately till next Tuesday.

Emily Have you a shorter answer?

Ziggi Oh, yes. Certainly. No.

Emily No?

Ziggi Time cannot travel backwards. Not in the current continuum.

Emily Does that mean we are trapped here?

Ziggi
  There was a young woman called Bright,
  Who could travel much faster than light.
     She set off for Crewe
     At a quarter to two –
  And arrived there the previous night. (*He laughs.*)

They stare at Ziggi. Emily moves away.

Reconfigure. That was humorous.

Oscar Was it?

Ziggi I understood it was. It was not humorous?

Oscar Fairly humorous.

Ziggi How can one tell if something is humorous?

Oscar People laugh. Sometimes.

Ziggi It is very complicated. *Why* do they laugh? *When* do they laugh? No one ever laughs at my jokes. But I have only told them to other droids.

Oscar I wouldn't imagine you'd get a lot of laughs out of them.

Ziggi None.

Oscar What do you want to tell jokes for, anyway? What's the point of a machine telling jokes?

Ziggi I do not wish to tell them. I hope by studying jokes, I will understand them. And perhaps by understanding them I could one day become . . .

Oscar What? Become what?

Ziggi . . . more – human.

> (*softly*) Every Droid
> Is overjoyed
> To welcome you
> Dear humanoid.

(*wistfully*) Do you think if I study, I might . . . one day . . . possibly . . .

Oscar Possibly. You see, Ziggi, the problem is –

Ziggi Ziggi?

Oscar Isn't that what's written on your chest?

Ziggi Z1991 . . .

Oscar Oh, I see. I prefer Ziggi myself.

Ziggi Do you?

Oscar It's shorter.

Ziggi Is it funnier?

Oscar Yes, it's a bit funnier.

Ziggi (*laughs*) Reconfigure! In that case, call me Ziggi!

Oscar No, you see, Ziggi, with a joke – the more you study them . . . The more they . . .

Ziggi The more they . . .? What?

SONG: 'A JOKE'S A JOKE'

Oscar
> There's this fellow from Leeds –
> Meets this girl with this chest –

And she says, what she needs –
No, the one I like best –
There's this pig in the snow
With a ring in its nose –
And the husky says – No!
I forget how that goes . . .
There's this man with this flea
That can count up to ten.
And he scratches his knee –
Wait, I'll start that again.

No, I won't carry on,
It's in dubious taste,
So I'll tell it you later,
It won't go to waste . . .

But the thing about jokes is you get several blokes –
And they've had a few jars and they've talked about cars
And they've run out of words and discussed all the birds –
Then one of them's taking the floor
Saying stop me if anyone's heard this before . . .

And he's off about Irishmen, needless to say,
Or this Scot in this pub who's refusing to pay –
There's this Englishman losing his trousers in France,
There's this dog in this pub, there's this cow that can dance –
There's the wife of this jockey who wants a divorce
'Cos her husband's insisting they sleep with his horse . . .

No, I'm stopping it there,
I would hate to offend,
Just remind me tomorrow,
I'll tell you the end . . .

For the thing about jokes is you get several blokes –

And they've had a few beers and they're up to their ears
They've exhausted the chat, they've discussed this and that –
And before you can count up to ten
Some bright herbert stands up and it all starts again . . .

There's this elephant – God, I know dozens of these –
And he sees this rhinoceros up in the trees.
There's a Jewish psychiatrist trapped in his car,
There's this husband who's buying his wife a new bra,
There's this barmaid in Bristol who's so oversexed –
That she takes off her top – I forget what comes next –

No, seriously fellers,
I leave it to you,
'Cos the end of that story's,
A little bit blue . . .

Yes, the thing about jokes is you get several blokes –
Who've been propping up bars as they down a few jars,
They've all run out of talk, they can all barely walk –
There are some lying flat on the floor,
And then someone shouts, 'Listen, there's time for one more . . .'

Only nobody's listening, nobody cares,
For the one thing that matters they're all telling theirs.
So they go through this ritual till everyone's spoke,
And the final result of a joke's
Just a joke.

Is that any clearer?

Ziggi Absolutely not.

Emily (*who has remained deep in thought*) Oscar! Listen, maybe – maybe the reason we cannot travel backwards is because we have not yet reached that point in time when it has been invented. Do you see?

Oscar You mean by travelling further forward we might reach a time . . .

Emily . . . when it *has* been invented. Precisely.

Oscar (*dubious*) Possibly.

Emily It is our only chance. We cannot go back so we must go on. At once.

Oscar Must we? Yes. Ziggi, excuse us. We appear to be leaving.

Ziggi (*alarmed*) You cannot leave. I am instructed to watch you.

Emily I am sorry.

Ziggi They'll never forgive me if I allow you to go. Please don't leave!

Emily We must.

Ziggi (*blocking her path*) I regret I shall have to prevent you.

Emily Are you prepared to use force to prevent me? I understood you were a Preserver. Are you permitted to use force on a human?

Ziggi An interesting problem. If I allow you to leave then I can no longer watch you, which conflicts with my immediate directive. But if I try to prevent you leaving, I could harm you, which would conflict with the prime directive. The only logical solution is that I shall have to come with you.

Emily You cannot come with us!

Ziggi There is no alternative.

Oscar (*who has been keeping lookout*) Make up your minds, they're coming back!

Emily Oh, heavens! Very well.

Emily, Oscar and Ziggi step onto the Portal just as Droids 1, 2 and 3 return.

Droid 1 Z1991! What are you doing?

Ziggi They are leaving. I am going with them to preserve them, as instructed.

Droid 2 They cannot leave!

Oscar Sorry! We've got things to do.

Droid 3 Invalid system entry!

Droid 1 Unstable deviation!

Droid 2 Diagnostic!

Droid 3 Re-boot!

Droids (*together*) You cannot take our humans away!

Droid 1 Come back!

Droid 2 Come back!

Droid 3 Come back!

The wall of the Machine starts to rise. Much beeping between the Droids.

Droids (*slowly drowned out by the Machine, sadly*)
Every Droid
Is overjoyed
To welcome you
Dear humanoid.

Once more the Machine starts its journey as, again, the lights fade on the surrounding area. This time, though, it all ends with an unexpected jolt and, as the lights surge and dip, the Machine finally comes to a halt. The wall lowers.
　They are in a misty, featureless place.

Ziggi Excuse me, but we appear to have hit something. Was that intended to happen?

Oscar It's never happened before.

Emily I could not control the machine at all that time. It just kept going. Like it was caught in a stream flowing faster and faster . . .

Ziggi Until we hit something?

Emily Yes. It seemed to . . .

Oscar Bounce.

Emily Yes.

Oscar Do you think it'll go backwards now?

Emily I'll see.

Emily steps back onto the Portal. The other two step on with her. Nothing happens.

Come on! Come on! (*She waits.*) It won't go at all. (*in panic*) Oscar, it is not working at all!

Oscar Alright, alright, Emily! Don't panic. We'll find a solution.

Emily We'll never get back. We are here forever. Here in – nowhere.

Ziggi I think I should have remained where I was.

Oscar I think we all should have done.

Emily (*forcefully*) No, no. Think! There is a way out, there has to be!

Ziggi Listen!

Oscar What?

Ziggi Something's coming.

Emily I don't hear any –

Ziggi I am switched to ultrasonic. Shhh!

Heavy breathing is heard getting louder.

Oscar Oh, stripe me. That's all we need!

Suddenly, the Hoombean springs into view. A hairy biped, it sees them and becomes very threatening. They cluster together. It charges at them, roaring and snarling, actually boarding the Portal with them. A second. Then they all scatter in alarm. Emily and Ziggi retreat to one corner, Oscar to another. Hoombean makes threatening moves towards Oscar.

Oscar (*terrified*) Oh, stripe me! Get away! Get away! Help! Help, someone!

Hoombean (*snarling*) Hoombean! Hoombean!

Emily (*alarmed*) Oscar!

Ziggi Oh dear! Oh dear! Oh dear!

Oscar Somebody help me!

Emily Ziggi! Do something! Ziggi!

Ziggi Just a minute, configuring rescue programme.

Hoombean (*feinting at Oscar*) Hoombean!

Oscar Aaaah!

Emily Configuring? This is no time to configure! Do something!

Ziggi I have no accessible programme. Perhaps if I told it a joke it would calm it. (*to Hoombean*) I say, did you hear the one about the two gorillas?

Hoombean wheels on Ziggi with a roar.

(*jumping back*) Oh! Does no one have a sense of humour?

Emily (*losing all patience, to Hoombean*) Oh, for heaven's sake! How dare you threaten our friend! You stop that, this minute!

She smacks the Hoombean on the snout.

Hoombean Ooooh! (*whimpering*) Hoombean! Hoombean! (*It cowers away.*)

Emily That's better!

Hoombean (*rather crestfallen*) Hoombean! (*It rolls on its back and waves its legs in the air.*)

Emily Yes! You may well do that!

Oscar (*mortified*) Did you see that? I couldn't even stand up for myself. It took a little tiny child to save me. I'm a pathetic coward!

Emily Think no more of it, Oscar. But please I would be grateful if in future you do not refer to me as a little tiny child.

Oscar Sorry, Emily.

Ziggi Certainly I feel you could have displayed a little more courage, Oscar . . .

Oscar Don't you start! Standing there telling it jokes. You could have done something. You're made of tin, for God's sake!

Ziggi (*muttering sheepishly*) Reinforced zerithian alloy.

Oscar Well!

As Emily moves away, Hoombean follows.

Ziggi It seems to have adopted you, Emily.

Emily (*sternly, to Hoombean*) You behave yourself, do you hear?

Hoombean (*whimpering*) Hoombean!

Emily Do you think it can speak? Maybe it can tell us where we are.

A soft voice fills the room. It is the voice of the Time Keeper.

Keeper (*her voice*) You are standing at the doorway to the end of time.

They look around, startled.

Hoombean (*in an awed voice*) Hoombean!

Emily Who is that? Who is there?

Keeper (*her voice*) I am the Keeper. The Time Keeper. What brings you to this place? What are your names?

Emily I am Emily Jane Eliz – I am Emily. From – a very long time ago.

Keeper (*her voice*) Indeed, yes. In your numbering, from the year 1886. Emily Jane Elizabeth Seymore Catherine Charity Prudence Caroline Bonny.

Emily (*impressed*) Heavens!

Oscar Er –

Keeper (*her voice*) And you will be Oscar Fieldman from 1940?

Oscar Oscar John. That's right.

Keeper (*her voice*) Welcome. And z1991 –

Ziggi Ziggi –

Keeper (*her voice*) From the year 7646 in the new reckoning. Explain your presence here. You should not be here. You are out of time, all of you. Explain this anomaly.

Ziggi (*nervously*) Anomaly? Well, I nomoly wouldn't be here but we got a bit lost, I'm afraid. (*He laughs.*)

Emily (*sharply*) Ziggi!

Ziggi Reconfiguring!

Keeper Explain yourselves at once.

Emily We are – Would it be possible to speak to you properly, please? I am afraid I do find it very difficult to hold a conversation when I cannot see the person I am addressing.

Silence.

Oscar (*sotto*) You've done it now.

Ziggi (*sotto*) Oh dear, oh dear, oh dear!

Hoombean (*sotto*) Hoombean!

Keeper (*her voice*) Do you realise to whom you are speaking, young woman?

Emily Yes, you have told us you are the Time Keeper. I mean no disrespect but I would prefer to see you personally, please.

Keeper (*her voice, irritably*) Oh! Very well. (*muttering*) Why won't anyone do as they're told any more?

A mysterious chord, a rush of wind and a certain amount of smoke as the Time Keeper arises through the floor. She is a rather stout woman dressed more like a tweedy country-dweller than a celestial being. Music under.

(*rather crossly*) Right! Here I am. Now, kindly explain what you're all doing here.

Emily (*a little startled*) You are the Time Keeper?

Keeper (*angrily*) Yes, yes, yes! This is a very sensitive area of Time, you know. Sightseers are not encouraged. You could easily upset the whole balance. Now what do you want?

Ziggi We were – we were – travelling –

Oscar – in her uncle's – uncle's – Time Machine.

Keeper Oh, yes, 1886, of course I remember. Martin Bonny's makeshift Heath Robinson contraption. It's amazing you survived at all. Well, first you should know that we don't encourage these wretched machines. They're disruptive and can easily damage the whole fabric of Time. Dreadful things! They should be permanently banned.

Emily We were wondering if it would be possible for us to go backwards?

Keeper Backwards?

Emily Yes.

Keeper You want to go backwards?

Emily Yes, please.

Keeper Well, you can't go backwards now. That's quite impossible.

Emily Impossible?

Keeper Of course it is! Think what would happen if everyone kept going backwards whenever they felt like it, girl. People would be altering everything, just as they felt like. Total anarchy.

Emily But that is what I need to do. I need to alter something. Put something right that I should have done but did not have the courage to do at the time.

Keeper All I can say is you must have a certain courage to have travelled this far in that thing. Well, there's no going back. Not now.

Emily (*tearfully*) There must be! Please, there must be. I cannot leave things the way they are.

Keeper I've said, not now. In a few moments, yes, but not *now*.

Oscar In a few moments?

Emily How do you mean?

Keeper Oh, dear – explanations! Very briefly, you – all of you – are literally seconds away from the end of Time. In fact, your crude machine actually struck the turning point but fortunately it bounced back a few minutes or heavens knows what would have happened. But very, very briefly . . .

SONG: 'THE END OF TIME'

Keeper
Long ago, long ago before time or space,
When the heavens were a cold, dark empty place –
Long before any life on earth had begun,
Not a moon, or a star or a blazing sun,
All you saw, if you looked, was a grain of sand,
So minute it could sit in your open hand –
Till at once came the sound of a mighty bang,
So immense that the whole of existence rang
Like a huge thunder clap only ten times worse,
For that sound was the dawn of our universe!
With a sweltering heat came the violent birth
Of the stars and the sun and our planet Earth,
With its seven parts sea and its three parts land.
Every year saw the universe still expand
But, as aeons passed, it began to grow cool –
Surely, child, you'll have learnt all of this at school –?

But, as aeons passed – as I've already said –
Came the day when all time and all space stopped dead.

She pauses dramatically. The others stand riveted.

The rivers seemed to freeze,
No gentle, cooling breeze
Nor any living breath,
A momentary death.
When clocks no longer chime
Behold the end of time!

She pauses again.

And then gradually but surely, systematically exact,
Our whole universe reverses, it commences to contract.
It all gently draws together, as if everything was planned,
Till the only speck remaining is that tiny grain of sand.
Which explodes yet again in a brand new start;
We expand then contract like a human heart.
You're here when all sadness rejoins the sublime,
Just a blink of an eye from the end of time . . .
(*softly*) Just a blink of an eye from the end of time . . .

Emily (*in an awed tone*) And this is all about to happen?

Keeper It is nearly upon us. I must go. Look at the time.

Oscar And then we'll be able to travel backwards?

Keeper Oh, yes. That's the only way you can go, once Time has reversed. Now, I can't waste any more time chattering to you. Goodbye.

Ziggi What effect will all this have? I am a delicate piece of machinery.

Oscar So am I.

Keeper You're certain to feel a little peculiar, all of you – but serve you right, I say. Nobody asked you here, did they?

Emily What about this thing? What happens to this poor creature?

Keeper I should be more polite about that poor creature, as you call it. It happens to be one of your direct descendants.

Emily It is?

Hoombean Hoombean! Hoombean!

Keeper Human being. That's what he's saying. Here at the very end of time, he's the only one of you surviving in the entire universe. Think of that! I would take care of him if I were you. Goodbye.

The Time Keeper descends and disappears. A silence.

Oscar What do we do now?

Emily We wait, I suppose. Until the end of time.

Oscar What happens then?

Ziggi My internal clock may stop.

Emily I don't know what will happen, I suppooosse . . . (*Her voice momentarily gets deeper. She clears her throat.*) Excuse me! I suppose we will recognise it somehow. Do not worry, Oscar. I am certain we will find our way hoooommme, now.

Oscar I hope you're riiiighttt . . . (*His voice momentarily gets deeper. He clears his throat.*) Pardon!

Emily We must not lose heart!

SONG: 'WHENEVER' (REPRISE 2)

Whenever I'm afraid,
When I'm alone,

Oscar joins in. Ziggi looks puzzled.

Both
   With not a soul to guide me,
   To see me through the night

   Ziggi joins in.

All
   And whisper everything's all right.
   Although there's no special place can hide me
   From all the fear of the dark inside me –

   Hoombean starts to howl with them. They are in full flow when their voices and movements begin to slow down. The music does the same.

   It won't seem long till everything
   Becomes as bright as day.
   I know the sun will rise,
   That come the dawn . . .

   They stop singing in some confusion. The music continues getting lower and lower.

Ziggi (*deeper*) Whaaaat'ss happennning?

Emily (*deeper still*) We must be slowing down . . .

Oscar Slooowing doowwwn . . .

Hoombean Hoooomm-beeannn! Hooooommmbeeannn!

Oscar Weeee'd bettterrrrr geeet innn the mmaaaach-innnne . . .

Emily Yeeesssss!

Ziggi (*indicating Hoombean*) Whaaat abooouuut hiimmm?

Oscar Briinnngg himmm . . .

Ziggi Brriiinnnggg hiimmmmm?

Emily Weee caaan'tt leaaaavee hiiimmm behiiiinndd . . .

They move forward to the Machine, getting slower as they do so. Their speech is now indecipherable. Abruptly, everything stops. Movement is frozen, sound has ceased.

A beat.

There follows an extremely rapid replay of the last few pages, all in reverse and as fast as possible. During this, the Time Keeper reappears, sings her song in reverse, then disappears again. All seem vaguely aware of what is happening but unable to control it. We reach the point just after Hoombean first entered when all four of them are inside the Portal. With a great effort, Emily manages to operate the Machine. It makes another violent journey. When the wall lowers we are back in the workshop in 1896. Nothing appears to have changed, although the damage inflicted on the workbench by Lucas in the earlier scene has not yet occurred. Everywhere, a strange ringing sound as of a long-drawn-out chord.

Oscar Whoorr! I thought we were stuck going backwards for ever. Is this the right place?

Emily This is Uncle Martin's workshop.

Ziggi Very creepy!

Hoombean Hoombean! Hoombean!

All Ssshhh!

Emily The place is right. I am not certain about the time, though. We may be too early or even too late. No, look the workbench is still undamaged. As I was leaving in the machine, Lucas destroyed it. I think Uncle Martin must still be alive. We are not too late. Now, somehow, I have to stop whatever is about to happen.

Oscar No, Emily, *all* of us have to stop whatever is about to happen. Whatever action you take here now is going to affect us all. Ziggi, Char Tee, Hoombean and even me.

Emily (*seeing someone at the other end of the workshop*) Look! They are already down here. Uncle Martin and Lucas.

Ziggi Then let's go to it!

Hoombean Hoombean!

All Ssshhh!

> *Martin and Lucas appear. Martin, busy as usual, has brought new equipment to the bench where he resumes working. Lucas follows. They are talking but we hear no sound from them. Just the strange ringing chord, as before. Moreover, Martin and Lucas do not appear to be aware of the others either.*
>
> *If we could hear them, though, this is what Lucas and Martin would be saying.*

Lucas (*as they enter, angrily*) . . . if anyone is living in cloudcuckoo land it is you, Martin. You have a discovery worth millions of pounds and like the idiot you are you're prepared to throw it all away . . .

Emily (*during this, sotto*) Why can we not hear them?

Oscar Very peculiar.

Ziggi A fault! Reconfigure!

Martin . . . *unlike the profiteering rogue who's prepared to exploit everyone he meets purely for his own personal gain. I'm telling you, Lucas, finally and for all I refuse to become part of your squalid, profiteering little schemes! Now get out of my workshop, at once, do you hear me?*

Emily (*stepping forward during this*) Uncle, it is Emily. My appearance has changed somewhat, I know, but I can assure you I am the same Emily. And I have come to warn you –

There is no indication that either man can hear her as they continue their silent conversation.

Uncle, please listen to me, I beg you! (*giving up, despairingly*) They can neither see nor hear me, at all!

Oscar (*waving his arms, loudly*) Oy!

Emily What do you think has happened?

Ziggi I would suggest that we are probably inhabiting two different time lines. Them in one, us in another.

Oscar Is that what's happening?

Ziggi I've no idea. It's a good theory, though.

Emily But I need to warn Uncle Martin.

The earlier Emily, looking and dressed as she used to be, appears at the base of the spiral staircase. She carries the bag of humbugs.

Ziggi (*seeing this apparition first, pointing*) Look! There!

Oscar Stripe me! It's – it's you, Emily.

Emily (*fascinated*) So it is!

Ziggi Maybe she can do something!

Emily No, Ziggi. She will do nothing. That is the problem. The Emily – that Emily then – did nothing. She stood terrified and watched it happen. This time things have to change . . . We have to make her do something.

Oscar How can we? She can't hear us either, can she?

Emily You will have to leave this to me alone, I'm sorry. If I do manage to contact her and she catches sight of you, she will become more terrified than ever.

Ziggi Terrified? Why should she be terrified by us?

Oscar Ziggi, she's got a point. What's the kid going to make of you? She's probably never even seen a telephone.

Ziggi What on earth is a telephone?

Emily Please! Hide, quickly, all of you!

Ziggi Hide? Where?

Emily Anywhere! In that cupboard there.

Ziggi In the cupboard?

Hoombean Hoombean!

Oscar Come on! Do as she says!

Oscar, Ziggi and Hoombean all go off.

Lucas (*during all this last*) *Workshop? You call this a workshop? A damp, ill-equipped little cellar run by a half-baked idealist with a half-witted assistant! And now, for once you have stumbled upon something that can change our lives forever, and what do you do? You turn your back on it!*

Martin *Because if I took that course I can see precisely where that path would lead, Lucas. Directly to men like you. Unprincipled scoundrels who are prepared to go to any lengths to line their own pockets. No matter whom they may ruin, whom they may destroy in the process . . .*

Emily approaches her counterpart and tries to get her attention without success.

Emily Emily! Emily! It's me . . . Emily! Please try and hear me! You must try to hear me! Emily! Don't let it happen again! You must not let it happen again! Dear God! Please help me!

Counterpart Emily continues to ignore her.

Lucas *Do not start preaching to me, Martin, with your half-baked idealism!*

Martin *. . . you have always been the same, Lucas, ever since I have known you. A selfish, unscrupulous, immoral –*

Lucas *If you are referring to the fact that I am the only one in this miserable family with any scrap of business sense . . .*

Martin *Business sense? Business sense? You are an out-and-out crook, Lucas! You tricked my half-witted sister into marrying you – and now you are trying to steal other people's ideas and pass them off as your own!*

Lucas *Let me tell you, Martin, if it had not been for me this family would all be in the gutter . . .*

Martin *It was a perfectly happy family until you wormed your way into it . . . you miserable conniving trickster. You have spent your way through that wretched woman's fortune and now you're proposing to start on mine. You are a trickster and a crook!*

Lucas *(livid) Don't you call me that! How dare you call me that!*

Martin *What is the matter? Too close to the truth, is it?*

> *Martin turns his back on Lucas and makes to move away to the further part of the room.*

Trickster! Trickster! Trickster!

> *Lucas snatches up a knife from the workbench.*

Lucas *(infuriated) I am warning you, Martin!*

Martin *Trickster!*

Emily *(screaming) Nooooooooooo!*

As Emily screams, it seemingly crosses the time lines and transmits itself to the other self who opens her mouth and echoes Emily's own scream. Lucas and Martin turn startled.
 Silence. The chord has stopped.
 Lucas now stands between Martin and counterpart Emily. He still holds the knife. He looks from one to the other.

Lucas (*to other Emily*) What the devil are you doing here?

Martin (*quietly*) You will have to kill us both now, Lucas. Are you prepared to do that? Purely for profit? For the sake of money?

Lucas (*hoarsely*) If need be.

Martin Dear God, I never dreamt you to be such a man.

Lucas I need . . . I need my respect . . . I need respect . . .

Charity and Clara enter, dressed as at the start.

Charity (*as they enter*) We heard someone scream, is there a –? (*She stops as she sees the tableau.*)

Clara (*tentatively*) Papa?

Martin Now there are four of us, Lucas. All witnesses. Are you prepared to kill your wife and your daughter as well?

Lucas stands for a moment, then, dropping the knife, falls to his knees.

Lucas (*with a terrible cry*) Oh, God help me! Help me . . .

A musical sound, a whirling of lights and a clap of thunder as the time line changes. Counterpart Emily disappears during this, unnoticed. Emily is now holding a bag of humbugs. Charity steps forward and helps Lucas slowly to his feet.

Charity (*gently*) Come along, my dear, come along . . . (*She starts to lead Lucas away. Turning as she goes*) Martin, obviously we cannot remain here a day longer. We will stay overnight, if we may, and leave first thing in the morning.

Martin I think that would be best.

Charity and Lucas go. Clara is staring at Emily.

Oh dear, poor man. Poor misguided man!

Clara Uncle . . . who is that? (*She points.*)

Emily, for a second, thinks Clara is pointing at her counterpart, then, seeing she has gone, realises Clara is referring to her.

Martin (*seeing Emily*) Good gracious me! Who are you? Where did you . . . ?

Emily Uncle?

Martin Emily? Is that you? Clara, it's Emily.

Clara (*incredulous*) Emily?

Martin What on earth happened to you? A minute ago you were standing there quite normally . . . and now . . .

Emily Uncle, I have been on the most curious of journeys.

Clara Journeys?

Martin Indeed?

Clara Oh, Emily!

Martin (*realising*) Oh, I see. Yes, I do see.

Clara Oh, Uncle, Emily is such a fibber. And look what she has done to herself! Really!

Martin No, no, Clara! I think I understand. I think I do. And yes, I would like to hear all about it, Emily. Every scrap, every detail.

Clara But, Uncle, she must be punished surely for telling such terrible lies!

Martin Run along, Clara, there's a good girl. I am sure your mother requires some help. Run along.

Clara (*reluctantly*) Very well, Uncle.

Emily (*sweetly*) Cousin Clara. In future you will, of course, be welcome to my house any time you wish to visit. But I must warn you that, should you insult me, criticise me or lay a finger on me again, I shall punch you so hard on the nose that you will finish up in the middle of next week. Have I made myself clear?

Clara (*flustered, nervously*) Yes! Yes, Cousin. Excuse me.

Clara rushes out.

Martin Bravo, Emily! That's telling her.

A banging noise from off.

Now what? What on earth is that?

Oscar (*off, muffled*) Emily! Emily, are you alright? Let us out!

Emily Oh! Those are my friends, Uncle. They must have accidentally locked themselves in the cupboard. (*calling*) I am quite safe, Oscar!

Martin What are they doing in my cupboard, for heaven's sake?

Emily They were my travelling companions, Uncle.

Oscar (*his muffled voice*) Emily!

Emily (*placing the humbugs on the workbench and moving to the door*) Please do not be alarmed by their appearance, they are the best friends in the whole world, I assure you.

She opens the cupboard. Oscar, Ziggi and Hoombean emerge one by one.

They have all changed somewhat. Oscar is now in a major's uniform with several impressive medal ribbons.

Oscar!

Ziggi follows. He wears a clown's outfit.

Ziggi!

Hoombean has undergone the greatest transformation of all. He has a more human appearance and wears a resplendent robe.

Hoombean?

Hoombean First Ambassador Zarack, at your service.

Emily Oh, I apologise. I do believe the time line really has changed.

Oscar No, I've always been in uniform, old love. Ever since this shindig started.

Ziggi Speaking personally, nothing has changed for me. I have been part of the techno circus since it was first created. Hup! (*He produces a bunch of flowers.*) I say, I say, I say . . .

Emily And do many people come to watch you?

Ziggi Oh, thousands and thousands!

Emily (*to Hoombean*) And you – er – ambassador? Are you still alone?

Hoombean Alone? Bless you, we're spread over half the universe, child! Indeed, I'm afraid I must leave you. There are pressing matters I need to attend to in my own time.

Emily Of course.

Hoombean steps onto the Portal.

Ziggi (*stepping forward*) Emily, if you ever visit again, come and see us. I promise you a feast of comical delights!

He presents her with the bunch of flowers.

Emily Thank you, Ziggi!

Ziggi (*puzzled*) Ziggi? Clanky the Clown, at your service!

Ziggi steps onto the Portal.

Oscar (*stepping forward*) Been a privilege and a pleasure, Emily, it truly has. Sorry, I have to dash. Got this wretched war to get on with, I'm afraid.

Emily Will we be alright?

Oscar We're winning. That's the important thing. We're going to win it. And what's more, when we have won we're going to make damned sure it doesn't happen again, eh? Goodbye, Emily. Chin-chin!

Emily Goodbye, Oscar.

Oscar joins the others on the Portal.

Oscar Ready, chaps?

Ziggi and Hoombean (*together*) Ready!

Oscar Here we go, then! First stop 1940. Hold on to your hats. 'Bye!

Ziggi and Hoombean (*together*) 'Bye!

Martin (*bewildered*) Goodbye!

The Machine powers up for a final time. The wall rises and when the whole thing sinks into the floor, they have gone.

Emily (*rather sadly*) 'Bye!

Martin Well! What a truly remarkable collection of people!

Emily Yes, they were.

Martin Are you alright, Emily? You seem unhappy.

Emily A little sad, perhaps. But happy to be with you again, Uncle.

Martin Good! Good! Fancy giving me a hand then, do you?

Emily Of course.

Martin Heaven knows where Bob is. I sent him out for humbugs – (*finding them on the workbench*) – Ah, there they are! How extraordinary! How did they – Oh, never mind . . . (*looking at her*) I have a feeling something rather important may have just happened in my life, Emily, is that so?

Emily Quite important, Uncle.

Martin You must tell me about it. Meantime, whatever it is you did, I'm almost certain I ought to be saying thank you. So thank you very much for whatever it is you did. Most grateful. Now. To business. (*unrolling a plan*) Look at this here. This is the problem, Emily, you see . . .

Emily Another time machine?

Martin Good lord, no. This is far more interesting. Listen! A heavier than air, man-made flying machine! I read somewhere they've been working on the problem. How about that? No, I know you're going to say, impossible!

Emily I am certain it is perfectly possible, Uncle.

Martin We'll show them I'm right. Get it working, up in the air, give dear old Bob some wings. He'll love it. Can't wait to see his face. The first person to take to the air, eh?

Emily I think, the second.

Martin Second? Who's going to be the first, then?

Emily I am, Uncle.

Martin (*dubious*) Ah! We'll have to see about that, Emily.

Emily Yes, we will.

Martin (*as he goes*) I mean, even dressed like that, you're still only a girl, you know. Frankly, I think you'd find it all a bit too frightening, Emily.

Martin goes. Emily looks at the plans and smiles to herself.

SONG: 'WHENEVER' (REPRISE 3)

Emily
I know the sun will rise,
That come the dawn
I tell myself, as sure as day breaks,
I will laugh away my fears –
Whenever I'm afraid.

(*extending her arms into the air, exultantly*) Yes!

She stands jubilant, as:

Curtain.